The Noble Anthony and His Lady Cleopatra

The Noble Anthony and His Lady Cleopatra

Paulette Gaines Wood

Noble Anthony and His Lady Cleopatra
Paulette Gaines Wood

Books may be purchased by contacting the publisher and author at:301-805-1805
aandc4321@gmail.com
www.flightsmedia.com

Cover Design: Beck Hastings
Interior Design: George Wood
Publisher: Flights Media
ISBN: 0692860436

ISBN: 9780692860434
Library of Congress Control Number: 2017903967
Paulette Gaines Wood,Bowie, MARYLAND

1. Cats 2. Dogs 3. Reincarnation 4. Ancient Egypt 5. Past Lives
First Edition
Printed in USA

There are many intelligent beings in the universe.

Most of them are owned by cats.

--From an old Polish proverb

Introduction

Anthony and Cleopatra

In the early spring, the mornings, just like the evenings, can still be rather chilly. This morning was like that—with a breeze blowing the new leaves on the trees and with a hint of moisture in the air from the rains the night before. Even though she was sitting on Anthony and not directly on the cold concrete, Cleopatra was sure that she could feel herself beginning to shiver.

"Anthony, My Beloved, it is cold out here. How much longer are we going to have to wait? I do not like this place."

"Not much longer, My Lovely," Anthony replied with his deep, gentle voice, lending reassurance to her as he always did. "Jennifer will be here shortly. She will let us inside, and you will be able to get nice and warm. Besides, at least your feet should be warm since you are sitting on me."

"I know my feet are warm thanks to you, but are you sure that this is the right place? Are you sure that this is where our new family will find us?"

"My Lovely, in all the centuries, have I ever been wrong about the location and arrival of a new family?"

"No, you have not. I just wish I had one of my coats. I do not have your body mass, and I am cold," she grumbled.

"Well, later today, The Lady Emma-Gene will come to us, and she will have a whole new wardrobe for you, which I am sure will include one or two new coats. Is that not worth waiting for?"

"Yes, I suppose that it is. Emma-Gene does make the most beautiful things for me," she remarked, as she reminisced fondly back on about the magnificent collar necklace made with green stones to match her eyes and the elegant golden cape that had been fashioned for her when she attended The Feasts of Bastet and presided over The Pronouncements. "But I still do not like this place. I hear fear, loneliness, and sadness coming from it."

"Listen more closely, My Love, and you will also hear the happiness of a loved one found and restored to the family or someone finally finding their forever home and a new family to love and care for them. There is a lot of happiness that also comes from this place, if you choose to see it. This is where our new family will find us. They are good people, and they have two wonderful boys."

Cleopatra could hear the glee in Anthony's voice at the thought of the boys he would get to play with and protect. Anthony loved children—all children, "Boys, more boys?" She was annoyed now.

"Now, My Dear Lady, you know you love children." Anthony was trying to be soothing.

"No, My Heart." Her voice was stern. "You love me, and I love you. You love children and especially boys, who are the worst, because with you, they will play, run, wrestle, and share their greatest joys and greatest sorrows. With me, they always want to touch me and rub my fur in the wrong direction. They want to sling me over their shoulder and carry me around like I'm a bag of laundry. They tend to have sticky hands, and they make a lot of noise, as if these ears could not hear a beetle walking across a leaf a half mile away if I wanted them to. They want to roughly rub my tummy, when it is well known that only The Special Ones are allowed to do that and only when I want a nice tummy rub. Now I will have to train another group how to be good humans. I tolerate the children—and these BOY children—because of you."

She had planned to continue this line of conversation but stopped short because, yes, that was the sound of a car tuning into the driveway. Maybe it was this Jennifer who would open the door and let them inside where it would be warm—or at least warmer than it was out here. Maybe it would not be much longer. She felt Anthony shift below her; of course, he was feeling the cold somewhat too. This Jennifer person needed to hurry up. The Noble Anthony, her sweet and wonderful Anthony, was indeed the protector of all children—if this was what made Her Anthony happy, then she would have to live with these humans and help him raise another litter of boys. No—humans did not have litters. Humans had this very inefficient way of having their young one—or two, maybe even three at a time. Anyway, she would help Her Anthony to teach them how to be good humans...and if for some strange reason they did not learn their lessons, she would turn them into geese. So then, in a few short weeks, they would be able to gracefully fly away and leave her alone and in peace.

"Oh, good." Now Cleopatra could hear footsteps coming toward the door. When it opened, she looked up into the face of a young woman who seemed nice enough, though obviously her mother had never taught her not to stare. The young woman in her nicely pressed uniform had the usual look of surprise most humans seemed to have the first time they saw her and Anthony, though Cleopatra had never been able to completely understand why.

When she and Anthony lived in The Temple, there had been litters for her to ride in and lots of servants to bear her. She had been able to lie on soft satin and perfumed pillows sheltered from the hot sun or a too cool breeze. Then she had been The Lady Cleopatra, and The Noble Anthony had walked beside her with pride. But that was then, and this new mode of transportation, riding on the head of Her Beloved where all could see them together, worked just fine. Her feet still did not touch the hard, rough, dirty ground. It would serve others well to try it before they condemned it.

Her train of thought was cut short when she realized that this Jennifer had said "good morning" and that she and Anthony had automatically and courteously bowed their heads in acknowledgment. Cleopatra was now hearing barks and meows coming from inside this place. The Noble Anthony had better be right that their new family would find them here—and soon—because nice young lady or not, she, The Lady Cleopatra, did not like this place. Not at all.

Jennifer

Jennifer loved her drive to work in the morning. Part of her pleasure was that she did not have to drive very far. Her job was only twenty minutes away from her house, and that was if she had to stop for every traffic light. The short trip was pretty nice, especially when she knew that some of her friends had to drive an hour or more to get to work. But, of course, they did not get to work in the same city where they lived.

The City of Bowie, Maryland, was a pleasant, small city surrounded by some pretty nice big cities. Many people liked to live there be, cause it was close to the nation's capital, Washington, DC; the state capital, Annapolis; and the big, busy City of Baltimore. This time of year, all the yards were bursting with the flowering colors of the new spring, so every street she drove down seemed like some kind of beautiful picture to her. Yes, the city itself was very pretty, but the main reason that Jennifer enjoyed her ride to work each day was that she loved where she worked, at The Bowie Animal Shelter.

All her life Jennifer had loved animals of all kinds. When she graduated from high school, she went to the local community college to learn to be a veterinary technician. She planned to become a veterinarian herself one day and have her own office. After she graduated from the college, she saw an ad in the local newspaper, *The Bowie Blade*, for an opening at the new animal shelter. She knew immediately this would be the perfect job for her. Now

Jennifer had worked at the shelter for almost two and a half years. She loved it because every day was new and different.

Most of the animals at the shelter were loved pets who had somehow managed to get separated from their homes. For these pets, whose families were looking for them, the reunions of humans and pets were wonderful. They involved lots of hugging, kissing, licking, and purring, and the people always said, "It's so good to see you again," and "We thought that we would never find you," and "Please don't ever do that again! We were so worried about you and lost without you." She got to see these kinds of family reunions almost every day.

Sometimes, though, a pet would be at the shelter for a while, and for some reason no one would come for it. That pet would be put up for adoption to go to a new family. Once again there was a lot of hugging, kissing, licking, and purring as a family found a new member to care for and love, and a pet would have a new forever home. The worst part, though, was when a family could not care for or keep a pet anymore, and they would bring it to the shelter so Jennifer and the rest of the staff could find it a new home. These times were rather sad, but Jennifer always knew that happiness would come again as soon as the pet found a new home. Once in a while, a family would feel so bad about not being able to take care of their pet that they would leave it at the back door of the shelter during the night. Jennifer would find the pet there in the morning when she arrived at work.

Once Jennifer arrived at work in the morning, she would hang up her keys, put her lunch into the refrigerator, and start the coffee for herself and the other staff members, who would arrive later. Then she would go to each cage to say good morning to each and every cat, dog, bird, lizard, mouse, rat, snake, or hamster who might be there. There would always be much tail wagging and head butting as they were all happy to see her again. She knew the names that had been given to each one, and she would stop and talk to every animal for a moment. Of course, in the morning, everyone wanted breakfast, but before she got the food, she had to go to the back door to see if anyone new had arrived.

New arrivals at the back door might be a box of kittens or puppies. Sometimes it would mean a dog tied up and waiting with its bowl and favorite toy or a cat in a carrier with its special blanket. That was what new arrivals usually looked like, so Jennifer was definitely not prepared for what she found when she opened the back door that particular morning. That morning she found a huge brown dog with a cat sitting on top of his head. The young vet tech, in her carefully pressed uniform, was greatly relieved none of her coworkers had arrived yet. She was very happy no one else could see her, because she was pretty sure that her mouth was hanging open in shock, surprise, and amazement.

The dog was large! Really, really large. Jennifer was sure that it must have weighed at least two hundred pounds. Its head and neck were massive—so much so that, had she felt the desire to throw her arms around him and hug him, she doubted that she could have reached all the way around him. Folds of soft wrinkles encased the face of the dog, almost hiding his eyes. Oh, his eyes! When Jennifer looked into the huge dog's deep bluish-brown eyes, she felt this wonderful wave of peace and love wash over her. For the first time in her life, she felt that she understood what love at first sight was all about, because there was no way to avoid loving those big, sad—but somehow, at the same time, happy and peaceful—eyes.

She moved her gaze on to the dog's legs, which were the size of big fireplace logs. They blended into huge feet that any good-sized giant would have been proud of. "Yes," thought Jennifer, "he must be a Mastiff, and from the shape of his head, probably an English Mastiff."

Mastiffs were one of the oldest of all the known dog breeds, and she was certain that they always had brown eyes and not the bluish-brown that this dog had. She smiled when she realized that the color of his eyes did not matter at all. Only what was in his heart mattered, and something told her that this big handsome guy would be a hero no matter what color his eyes were.

The huge dogs could be fierce fighters. The ancient Romans would put armor on them and take them into battle. At the same time, they were also gentle giants who were loyal, loving, big couch potatoes and protective pets who made a wonderful addition to any family.

Finally Jennifer noticed the thick brown leather collar around the dog's massive neck, which she was sure was larger than her own waist. Attached to the leather was a bright silver band, and even from where she stood, she could read the word "ANTHONY."

"Well, good morning, Anthony. I have to say that you are one big and very handsome boy. And who is your rather strange friend?"

Strange was the only word that Jennifer could think of. She had never seen a cat sitting so perfectly balanced on top of a dog's head before. Even a dog with a head as large as this one. The cat was beautiful, with a narrow, chiseled triangular face and very high cheekbones. The large ears were also triangular, and Jennifer could see them rotating like satellite dishes, taking in the sound of her every word. The eyes were large, almond shaped, and green. In fact, on closer inspection, the eyes appeared to be three distinct shades of green, going from light green on the outer edge to the deepest emerald green in the center. The single color "brown" could not begin to describe the cat's coat. It was a magical mixture of reddish, golden, amber, and brown, all blended into a much more perfect *brown*. Jennifer guessed that it was probably an Abyssinian. Abyssinians were also one of the oldest lines of cats, dating back to the times of the Egyptian pyramids and ancient Romans. If the ancient Romans had wanted to send a cat into battle, Jennifer was pretty sure that this cat would have been able to take care of herself and quite a few of the enemies too. This cat was not like any other that she had seen before.

First of all, this cat was wearing jewelry—and a lot of it too. Large gold hoops hung from the lower part of her ears. Then the collar, which looked more like a necklace, spread brightly colored stones out around the cat's neck and over her chest. There were wide gold bands like bracelets on the lower front legs, and a large green stone sat on top of one paw like some kind of ring. No, no one had seen an Abyssinian—or any other cat, for that matter—like this before...unless maybe...Jennifer tried to remember where she might have seen cats dressed like this before. But what she had just remembered could not be right. Had she seen cats dressed like this in pictures of the walls of the ancient Egyptian pyramids and temples? And if that was right, why was this cat dressed like them? Well, Egyptian temples or not, it was time to get them inside.

Jennifer's eyes searched at first slowly and then more frantically for the leash or rope that had to be attached to Anthony. When he was left outside the shelter, The Big Mastiff had to have been tied to something so that he would not run away or try to follow his family back home, but there was no leash. There was no rope. So, could he have somehow found his way to the shelter on his own? Wherever the dog had been before he arrived at the back door, he seemed to have been well cared for and well fed. And the cat—the cat was definitely where she wanted to be, sitting right there on the dog's head. Somehow Jennifer was beginning to feel that this strange pair had always been together and that they had always traveled this way. Jennifer knew for sure her friends were never going to believe this one.

⌒⑂⟆

"Well, Anthony, since you're here, would you and your friend like to come in and have some breakfast with us?" Jennifer asked. The big dog almost seemed to smile at her. As he stood up, the cat kept perfect balance on his head, and they moved as one unit into the hall. She gave a quick glance around the rest of the area to be sure that there were no other arrivals, because after seeing these two, she had completely forgotten the possibility that there could be any others. Thankful that the dog and cat were the only ones, she closed the door behind them and led them down the hall.

The shelter did not keep dogs and cats together, and all new animals were kept away from the others until the shelter vet could check them to make sure that they were healthy and did not have anything that might spread and harm the other animals. Also, before they could be adopted, all dogs and some cats had to be tested so the shelter could make sure that they would be good and safe pets.

Dogs would go into rooms where they would have a bed to lie on, bowls for food and water, and access to the outside so that they could get sunshine and go to the bathroom. Each dog room had a large glass window in it so that the staff could check on the animals. The window also allowed prospective new parents to see the dog without going into the room. Cats were put into cages according to their size, and each contained a bed, food and water bowls, a litter box, and one or two toys for them to play with.

Jennifer was thankful that they had one room left that was large enough for Anthony, and on a nearby shelf, she saw a good-sized animal carrier that she could put the cat into in order to take it to the cat area. As she turned away from them to get the carrier from the shelf, she said absentmindedly, "Just a moment, guys, while I get this for the cat." She took the carrier from the shelf and then reached out with the other hand to pick up the cat. Then in mid-reach, her body seemed to be frozen in place, and she felt a chill run down her back. Something or someone seemed to be holding her in place—something or someone with very large green eyes.

Though it was only a second or two, to Jennifer it felt like forever before she could get her body to move again. She looked around, and as she expected, no one was there. She could only wonder, "What the heck was that?"

She turned back, and there was Anthony, with his strong handsome face and with that strange cat sitting on his head. That cat with the green eyes. Jennifer heard a voice saying something. It had to be her voice because none of the other employees had arrived at the shelter yet, but the voice was saying such strange things. Things that she would never say.

The voice was saying, "You know, I don't think I'm going to try to move this cat. You guys just look like you belong together, and it would probably be a lot less stressful for both of you if you stayed together right now." And less stress for herself, she thought, but not even the voice that was not hers dared to say that aloud. "You two sure look like you're good friends, and what harm could it do for you to stay together for a while?"

She held the door open for them, and they walked into the room. Once inside, the two turned to face her, and the dog sat down with the cat still in place. Jennifer looked into the green eyes, and for a moment, she thought the cat's head had nodded in her direction, as if it were agreeing that she had made the right decision by letting them stay together. Then the cat nodded again, as if giving the young woman permission to leave the room.

Jennifer closed the door behind her and gave an audible sigh of relief. She did not look back at the pair. The other animals were going to have to wait a few more minutes for their breakfast that morning. Jennifer desperately needed to have some coffee first and hoped that her hands would stop shaking. She might even begin to reevaluate her choice of career.

Emma-Gene

It was late, and she was tired, but there was still too much to do for her to stop anytime soon. This was far from the first late night she had spent in her sewing room. She used the big upstairs bedroom of her Cape Cod house as her sewing room. The room had the sloping walls of an attic, so she could not have the tall storage shelves she had always wanted, but it was still the largest bedroom in the house. She had found that her four-foot shelves, which almost circled the room, worked just fine. For such a big room, it had only one very small closet, so it was the shelves that held bolts of fabric, baskets and boxes of patterns, threads of all colors, sewing-machine parts and feet, buttons, ribbons, tapes, many sewing gadget must-haves, sewing books, magazines—you name it, and, if it had to do with sewing, Emma-Gene had it. To the amazement of many others, she still managed to find room for a cutting table, three different kinds of sewing machines, and two different dress forms. Sewing was one of the few things Emma-Gene had been able to do well her entire life. In fact, she could no longer remember a time when she had not been able to sew.

⌒⫟⌒

Like many women of her age, which she liked to tell people was somewhere between twenty-five and three hundred, she had begun her sewing career by making doll clothes by hand. At first she created clothes for the usual baby or infant type of doll, and later, as she grew up, she moved on to the more grown-up, adult-looking dolls. Once in a while, her mother would buy her patterns, but they were expensive, so most of the time she would use notebook paper, a tape measure, a pencil, and a pair of scissors to make her own patterns. Her mother liked to tell friends that her daughter had begun by hand sewing very tiny but very straight stitches. By the time Emma-Gene was six, she had moved on to the family's old Singer sewing machine. From there it had not taken many steps before she was making aprons, skirts, and a couple of simple dresses. Then after a few trips to the library, and with the help of the good sewing books she found there, she had moved on to making and designing coats, gowns, curtains, and bedspreads. This was all before she left high school.

There had never been any thought of her going to college or having a real *career*, because at that time, girls were supposed to get married, and their husbands would have the careers and take care of them. Having a husband might have been all right for some girls but not for her, because by the time Emma-Gene had finished high school, she had already developed a great reputation throughout the community as a Professional Seamstress. It was a title that she had worn with pride for many years, and she had been able to make a very nice career for herself doing what she loved. She did not need a husband to take care of her because she could take care of herself.

Some of the work she did for people included alterations like hemming or taking in a dress or a pair of pants. She might even put a new zipper into a jacket. That was OK, but what she really loved to do was to make gowns. She made nightgowns, bridesmaids' gowns, and gowns for flower girls, first communions, and baptisms. There were also prom gowns, pageant gowns, gowns for both the mother of the bride and the mother of the groom, and, of course, wedding gowns. It had even been rumored that a certain European Royal Family had contacted her about making the wedding gown for their son's bride.

She was not making any of those that night. That night she was sewing something very special for someone very special. Emma-Gene was putting the finishing touches on a beautiful gold robe encrusted with a huge collar of multicolored jewels. Its diminutive size did not take away from all the time, work, and love she had put into this garment. Some unknowing person looking at it for the very first time might think that Emma-Gene had begun to make doll clothes again. After all, it was not all that hard to find the two shelves in the room that had been completely dedicated to these doll-like clothes.

These shelves held robes of all colors, coats, hats, headdresses, boots, earrings, necklaces, and rings of all kinds. All were in the same tiny size, but none of them were for a doll. This wardrobe was way too important and elegant for any doll. Emma-Gene would work long into the night to complete these pieces by daybreak for a very special lady, who would be arriving shortly with her faithful companion. There was no time to waste, for The Lady could not be kept waiting. It would be, as always, an honor to serve her again.

Emma-Gene gave a little sigh of pleasure and satisfaction while pushing a random curl of hair away from her eyes. It had been a long time since she had been given the pleasure and honor of sewing for My Lady, and now things were finally once again as they should be.

The Family

"Let's hurry up with breakfast; I want to be at the shelter right after they open this morning. I don't want anyone to take our dog before we get there, because today we're not going to get a cat, and we're not going to get a hamster or a goat. We're going to bring home a dog! A BIG DOG!"

The Father, Michael Wilkinson, could hardly contain his excitement. The Wilkinson family was finally going to adopt their dog. Michael had wanted a dog for years. He had grown up with dogs, and for most of his life, he had slept with something that had four legs and a tail. That is, until he met, dated, and married his wife, Michelle. His first dog had been a big yellow Labrador Retriever named Samson. Samson had been very large for a Lab, and his size had just made for more of him to love. Through his entire time with Michael, he had been as loving, loyal, and playful a companion as any boy could have ever wanted.

Samson was followed by Simba, the Great Dane. Simba had been a hundred and fifty pounds of ridiculousness. The big, silly dog was a fawn brown that changed into a soft black mask on his face. This dog, who weighed as much some grown men, would constantly try to climb into the lap of anyone who was unfortunate enough to be sitting down at the time. He attempted to do this by pressing the flat part of his face into the person's chest and then trying to put one of his hind legs onto the chair. This never worked.

He would also sit on the couch with his rear end on the seat and his feet on the floor, as if he were a person.

Michael's parents did not want the dog to sleep on their son's bed, so Simba would sneak onto His Boy's bed. He was tall enough that the corner of the bed would fit under his chest when he was standing. Then he would move over far enough to pull one of his back legs onto the bed. Then a front leg, and before anyone knew it, a mountain of brown fur would be snoring away on the bed, and no one would know how he got there or even notice him—at least that was the way it worked in Simba's mind.

Life with the huge Dane was always interesting. Once he dug a hole in the backyard, so deep that he could hide in it and then jump out to frighten the unknowing friend, neighbor, or passerby half to death. He loved carrots, and once he ate some orange candles, thinking that they were carrots. He would crawl under the kitchen table and then decide to stand up, lifting the table on his back, while his humans scrambled to hold on to plates and glasses. The Father could remember many a night sleeping on the floor beside his bed because the huge Dane had completely taken it over. These were the experiences that he wanted his sons, Jeffrey and Bobby, to have. He wanted his boys to know the joy of living with a *BIG DOG*.

Michelle Wilkinson, The Mother, had always been concerned about having such a big animal in the house when her sons were very little, even though her husband had tried to reassure her many times that big dogs could be especially gentle with children. She had suggested that he could have a *BIG DOG* around all the children that *he* personally gave birth to, because it was not going to happen with *her* babies until they were older. She wanted them to at least have a fighting chance if the family dog felt the need to sit on them. Now that Jeffrey was ten and Bobby was seven, she had finally given in. This sent her husband straight out to The Big Giant Pet Store to get ready for his *BIG DOG*. The Mother had not thought about that part.

They bought two beds for him or her. The Father did not care if his *BIG DOG* was male or female. There also had to be a raised food stand because it was not good for large dogs to lean down too far when they ate. To go with the stand, they bought two stainless steel bowls for food and water. The bowls actually were closer to the size of the tubs that people bathed their babies in rather than to the size that The Mother made pancakes in. Next came the collar, which was so long that The Mother fastened it around her waist and asked her husband just how BIG this *BIG DOG* was going to be.

When The Father began to look for a leash to go with the collar, The Mother suggested maybe they should be looking at the kind of rope that people used to tie up their boats, saying that should be big and strong enough. The Father chose to ignore her. He was struggling under the weight of a bag of dog food that was bigger than both The Boys put together, and they still had to go to the aisle with all the dog toys. Three full shopping carts later, they were almost ready to check out. The Father only had one last thing to get, and that was a name tag for his BIG DOG to wear on his collar. It would read "Igor." That was going to be the name of his dog—well, maybe "Igorina" if it did happen to be a girl. The Father announced that to almost everyone in the store who was polite enough to listen.

He had been so caught up in his shopping frenzy that he never noticed his wife had left him and quietly wandered off to The Cat Aisle. The Mother had always wanted a cat. She had never had one and had always been completely captivated with them. The beautiful eyes, the soft lulling sound of the purring, and the cuddly warmth you could hold in your arms or on your lap. Yes, a cat would be wonderful, but she had married a man who loved dogs, so that was what they were going to get. A dog. *A BIG DOG.*

⌒⋀⋂⊤

Breakfast was over, and the kitchen had been cleaned up, so it was finally time to go. They all climbed into the family van and headed off to The Bowie Animal Shelter. When they arrived, a young woman in an official-looking uniform was sitting behind the counter, sipping on a cup of coffee. Her hands might have been shaking just a little bit, but she greeted them with a smile and a voice that tried very hard to be cheery. "Hi, my name is Jennifer. How may I help you today?"

The Father was very quick with his answer. "Well, good morning, Jennifer. We are the Wilkinson Family. I'm Michael. This is my wife, Michelle, and these are our two boys, Jeffrey and Bobby, and we are here this morning to adopt. We don't want a cat. No, no, we're not a cat family. We're a dog family, and we want A BIG DOG. So, Jennifer, I'm hoping that you have A BIG DOG for us to take home with us this morning.

"Well, Mr. Wilkinson..." Jennifer's words came slowly because she could not help but be a little hesitant as her mind quickly went to the two newest guests in the room just down the hall. "We have several good family dogs here that you might like. We don't very often get dogs of the size I think you're talking about, but we did have a new arrival just this morning."

"Great! Let's go and take a look at it." The Father was so excited as if he expected the dog to suddenly appear right in front of him.

"Unfortunately, Mr. Wilkinson, this dog is so new that our vet hasn't had a chance to see him yet. We don't consider any animals to be ready for adoption until they have been examined by the vet so you can be sure that you are not taking home a sick animal that might endanger your family. Also, all dogs have to be tested so we know they will be good family pets. We need to know they are not overly aggressive or overly protective of their food. We need to know if they will be safe to be in a home with children or if maybe they should go to a home of all adults. We have to know how they will react to cats or even other dogs that might already be in the family." With a voice that was friendly but at the same time determined, she went on, "When an animal leaves the shelter, we want to be as sure as we can that it will be the right fit so that its new home will truly be a forever home for it. So we need to spend a certain amount of time with the animal to be able to do that. Also I think that I should tell you that this dog arrived with a cat, and they seem to be very..." Jennifer paused, not quite sure how to explain the obvious bond between the pair in the room down the hall. "Let me just say that they seem to be very, very attached to each other."

The Father was a little surprised by the cat part, and it showed, but he did manage to recover quickly. "We're not interested in the cat, but we definitely want to see the dog."

"Well, I wouldn't mind seeing the cat." The Mother quietly slipped into the conversation. She responded to her husband's furrowed look with a few simple words. "It couldn't hurt to take a look at the cat." Jeffrey and Bobby looked at each other and then shrugged their shoulders, choosing to ignore both their parents.

"Sure, follow me." Jennifer led The Family down the hall to the room that had the large glass window in the door and let them look inside. At first they all just stood and stared into the room. All four members of The Family seemed to be struggling to understand what they were seeing.

Jennifer went on, "As you can see, I wasn't kidding when I said that the dog and the cat seem to be attached to each other." Yes, there they sat, just as she had left them. It was almost as if they had known not to get too comfortable because someone would soon be coming for them. The big dog was there, with the jewelry-wearing cat still sitting on his head. Since the Wilkinson Family seemed to be seeing them too, the dog and cat must be real. It also meant that everything that had happened that morning had been real too. The uncomfortable part of it was that she still did not know whether their being real was a good thing.

Jeffrey, the older of the boys, was the first to find his voice, and it was filled with awe. "Dad, isn't that the biggest and most wonderful dog you've ever seen? He must weigh more than Bobby and me put together. And look at his eyes. You can just look into his eyes and know he's a good dog. Wow, he is so cool. But I don't know why that cat is sitting on his head like that."

The Mother was next to speak, and she had the same sound of awe and wonder in her voice. "Oh, Michael, isn't that the most beautiful cat you've ever seen? Look at the eyes. I don't think I've ever seen eyes like that on a cat before. They look like they're at least three different shades of green. And the way that she looks at you, it's almost as if she knows what you're thinking." Then, just for a moment, The Mother's own brown eyes seemed to sparkle with a hint of green, and her voice dropped almost to a whisper. "She's simply beautiful. I want her. I want to take The Lady Cleopatra home with me."

"I want to take the cat home." Those were the words Michael Wilkinson thought he heard his wife say. "No. No cat. We came for a dog, and that's what we're going home with: A *DOG*. So let's go in and meet the dog. And I'm saying this for the very last time: *THE CAT IS NOT COMING HOME WITH US!"*

On the ride home, The Father was still wondering exactly what had happened back there and where it had all gone so horribly wrong. He looked over at his wife, who was sitting beside him in the front seat. Sitting in her lap was a golden-brown cat wearing jewelry, and she had the strangest green eyes he had ever seen. For a moment, as the green eyes looked back at him, he even thought that he heard a voice saying, "All is as it should be," and there was a smile in that voice. No, he was hearing things. It had to be something one of The Boys had said. Of course, it was; that had to be it. Jeffrey or Bobby must have said it. Well, that was a relief, even though Michael Wilkinson was pretty sure he had never heard either of his sons talk like that before.

The Father tried hard to think back to Jennifer and the shelter. What had happened back there? He said that they would take the dog but not the cat. He was pretty sure about that part. Jennifer said that the dog could not leave yet because he had not been seen by the vet or been tested to be sure that he would be safe with a family. She also kept going on about how she did not think that the dog and cat should be separated from each other.

Then his wife, for some reason, said that she wanted the cat and that she would call her Cleopatra. After that someone, but not Jennifer or one of The Boys, said that the dog would not go without the cat and that they had to stay together. Who had said that? From what he could remember, no one else had been there.

He knew it was his voice that had said, "Well, I'll be happy to sign a paper saying that I accept full responsibility, that my family will be safe with the dog, and that we'll take them both to the vet straight from here." Why had he said that? He had said they would take *BOTH* of them, the dog *AND* the cat. While still at the shelter, he was so busy wondering why he had promised to take both of them that he almost missed Jennifer saying the dog would have to be on a leash and the cat would have to be put into a carrier in order to leave the building.

The Father knew for sure this next part happened, because even thinking about it sent that same cold chill throughout his body again. All three adults and even Jeffrey and Bobby turned and looked at each other. The look on all of their faces was that of *FEAR*. The fear of putting the cat into a carrier froze all of them in place where they stood.

Once again he heard that voice—the voice of the other person he could not see. "The cat will be just fine if your wife holds her in her lap." Who had said that? But somehow the paperwork had been filled out and signed. They had received their New Pet Parent Package and the name of a veterinarian called Dr. Daisy. The good part came when they had all left the shelter together and The Father had *THE BIG DOG* that he had always wanted. Of course, the dog's name was going to be Anthony and not Igor as he had wanted, but that was OK. That was fine. He was not sure the other part was so good, because he had somehow left the shelter with a cat named Cleopatra, a cat that he had said he did not want. How had that happened?

Well, however it had happened, it was done now. When The Father looked into the rearview mirror, he could see Jeffrey and Bobby hugging and petting the dog, whose huge body was stretched out between them on the back seat of the van. The Boys were busy talking about all the things that they would do together with their new friend, and smiles and laughter had completely taken over their faces. Looking at them, The Father had to smile to himself in pure satisfaction. Yes, seeing his sons so happy with their new BIG DOG —well, maybe this was as it should be. Of course, there was still the problem of that ridiculous cat.

Dr. Daisy and Suzanne

"You know, Michelle," The Father said, looking at his wife thoughtfully and all knowingly, "I'm very glad that Jennifer was able to get us an appointment for the animals with this Dr. Daisy right away. The Boys are here, and they can begin to learn about their animals and how to care for them."

"Ouch." The Mother had felt Cleopatra's claws suddenly dig into her thigh when her husband said the word "animals." She immediately reached out to give the cat a reassuring pat. "It's all right, my dear. I'm sure that he didn't mean to call YOU an animal." The Mother shot her husband a sideways if-looks-could-kill glance while still calming the cat and saying, "We all know that you are a cat and not an animal. You are our Cleopatra." Again her voice softened, and if her husband had not been paying attention to the road, he might have seen the little green flicker in his wife's eyes again as she continued, "You are our lovely Lady Cleopatra."

The Father did turn and look at this wife in absolute horror. "Michelle, what are you saying? Did you hear what you just said? She's a cat. A do-nothing, hairball-barfing cat, and the last I heard, dogs, as much as I love them, and do-nothing cats were both considered to be animals. Especially cats. We are not going to have any of this nonsense over an animal. Even Igor—I mean Anthony—is still a dog, and he always will be a dog." He turned his head back to the road, but since he heard no protest from his wife, he looked back in her direction to be certain of his triumph on the subject. This time his eyes locked, not with his wife's but with the green eyes of the cat, and then he heard the voice. The funny thing was, he would tell himself later, it sounded like his voice, but it could not have been his voice because of what it said. This voice said, "But this cat is different. This cat is special." The Father suddenly felt all the eyes in the van on him, and it was a very uncomfortable feeling. To try to distract everyone, including the cat, he said, "Oh, look. I think this is our turn. We're almost there. The vet's office should be right about here."

⌒⋀⋔⋀⋒

Dr. Daisy had never been so glad to have an appointment canceled before. She would have to remember to always give herself some time after the triplets came in. She needed some time after Cathy (for Catherine the Great of Russia), Lizzie (for Elizabeth I of Great Britain), and Mary (for Mary Queen of Scotland) had been in for their checkups. She needed some time to sit down for a few minutes with a cup of tea. The parents of the triplets were very nice people, but who would go to a breeder to get one Saint Bernard puppy and go home with three of them? Who would do that? When the triplets first came to Dr. Daisy, they had been just eight weeks old and had already weighed about 30 pounds each. Now they were two years old and 160 pounds (Cathy), 155 pounds (Lizzie), and 150 pounds (Mary) of jumping, kissing, slobbering, barking, and shedding, all at the same time. It was not that the parents were not nice or that the dogs themselves were not sweet and loving; it was just that there was so much of them.

"Gather yourself together, Daisy, old girl," she thought. "Have your tea. Maybe do some of your paperwork and remember why you wanted to be a vet in the first place." Daisy could not think of a time when she had not wanted to take care of animals. Being a vet and having her own office were all she had thought of when she was growing up. Getting married and having her son had interrupted things a little bit, but when old Dr. Pat, whom she had been working with, decided that it was time for her to retire, Daisy was ready to go for it. The icing on the cake was that Suzanne, Dr. Pat's vet tech, wanted to stay and work with her. It was perfect. They worked well together, and they built a very nice little business while bringing all kinds of animal babies into the world, teaching their human parents how to keep them healthy so that they would have long lives, and crying with those parents as they said their last good-byes to the pets they had loved and cared for.

When she was ready to enjoy a few quiet moments after the triplets, the phone rang. Dr. Daisy decided to let Suzanne answer it because she was enjoying her tea and was planning to take her shoes off. Oh, and after being with The Slobbery Three, she needed to change her lab coat too. "Dr. Daisy, it's Jennifer from The Bowie Animal Shelter, and she needs to talk to you right away."

Well, the idea of a moment or two of quiet time had been a nice thought while it lasted. Dr. D reached for the phone. "Yes, Jennifer, what's going on?"

"I hate to do this to you, Dr. D, but I have a family I've pointed in your direction after an adoption of a dog and a cat this morning. Dr. Tom, our vet, won't be in until later this afternoon because he's doing some family thing with his kids. This family, The Wilkinsons, especially the dad, was insistent about taking them right away. I just found the dog and cat at the back door this morning, so no one but me has seen them yet. They probably wouldn't believe what they saw anyway. Let me just say, this pair, this dog and cat, is rather...I'll just say 'special.' I need your help."

Dr. Daisy had been working with The Bowie Shelter since they first opened. She loved the work that they did, and she loved and respected their staff. Both sides had been able to help each other out many times, so it never would have occurred to her to not do whatever they needed. Besides, she could hear and almost feel the stress in Jennifer's voice. Whatever was going on, she knew that she had to help. "It's fine. Don't even think about it. I've had a spot open up that I wasn't expecting, so if they're on their way, that should be perfect."

No one could have missed the sigh of relief in Jennifer's voice as she said, "Oh, thank you so much. I owe you for this. In fact, I may have to take you to lunch so that we can talk about this one."

"Not to worry, dear. We will make it work. I'll check back with you if there are any problems." Sure, the doctor told the tech not to worry. She had confidence in herself, her education, her experience, and the fact that this was going to be a routine checkup. But if that was the case, why was she beginning to feel worried?

～〜

Jeffrey had put Anthony on the bright red leash The Father had bought for his Igor, and it looked very handsome on Anthony. The Mother carried Cleopatra, gently holding her close against her chest as they entered the vet's office. The waiting room was bigger than they had expected. The big floor-to-ceiling windows in the front let in plenty of sunlight, so the room had a nice cheery look to it. Most of the pictures on the walls were of the many pets that Dr. Daisy had cared for: dogs, cats, turtles, hamsters, ferrets, hedgehogs, gerbils, lizards, a falcon, and a snake or two. The chairs and benches all around the walls would allow plenty of room for separation if needed. The Boys and The Mother all found seats on one side of the waiting room while The Father once again filled out New Pet Parent Paperwork, but this time it was for the veterinarian. The Mother tried to hold Cleopatra securely—but not too securely—on her lap. She was afraid of what might happen if another animal, especially a strange dog, came into the office. In her heart, she knew that she was wondering what might happen to the dog.

The thought had hardly left her when another family, with a mother, a father, and a daughter, came in with a black female Labrador Retriever. The two families nodded politely to each other, and the Labrador's family took seats on the other side of the waiting room. The Father immediately sat up a little taller and smiled because he knew he had the THE BIGGEST DOG in the room.

"What kind of dog is that?", the other father asked.

Delighted by the question, The Father puffed himself up with pride and answered, "He's an English Mastiff. They're one of the oldest breeds known, and many other breeds are based on them. In fact the Romans used to put armor on them and take them into battle." Again, he felt his family's eyes settle on him in wonder. How did he suddenly know so much about English Mastiffs? They had gone to the shelter in search of a, not any particular kind of, BIG DOG. Under the disapproving look of his family, The Father felt the need to change the topic. "Anthony here doesn't have to worry about anything like that," he said, trying to force a laugh while giving him a pat on the head. For once, Cleopatra was not sitting on it. Thank goodness. "No, Anthony is just going to be a good family pet and maybe a little bit of a guard dog."

As the two men continued to talk, the black Lab, who was on an auto stretch leash held by her human father, started to inch her way closer to where The Mother sat. She took a quick look at Cleopatra sitting on The Mother's lap, sucked up air, and then snorted it out through her nose in a way meant to dismiss the cat's presence. Cleopatra gave the dog a cold stare.

The Mother felt claws coming through the fabric of her pants for the second time that day. This time she petted the cat and whispered to her, "It's all right, My Lady. That animal is not going to bother you."

The Lab, thinking that she had dismissed the cat, moved over to Anthony. Smiling and vigorously wagging her tail, she looked up into his big face and said, "Hi, my name is Tara Tupa, and I've never seen a dog as big and handsome as you are. What's your name?"

Anthony's huge head moved slowly so he could look down at the smiling, wriggling, wagging mass of black fur in front of him. "My name is Anthony, and I am The Beloved Husband of The Lady Cleopatra." He turned his head and nodded in Cleopatra's direction.

Tara Tupa laughed at him. "You have got to be kidding me. You mean you are the husband to a cat? That cat right there? Don't they have any dogs where you come from?" Suddenly the Lab was not smiling or wagging anymore. Against her will, she felt her head being pushed down into the submissive dog pose, and then her tail was forced between her back legs, which were bending into a bow. Then most humiliating of all, she heard herself begin to whimper.

At the same time, she heard the cat's voice saying, "Of course, The Noble Anthony is my husband, and he has been my husband for all the ages past, and he will be so for all the ages to come. I trust that this news gives you some kind of distress and sense of loss." Again, the Lab whimpered, and this time she began to back away. "Yes, return to your humans and stay there," commanded Cleopatra.

Tara Tupa turned around and ran back to her humans, almost pulling the leash out of her human father's hand. She frantically tried to climb up into her mother's lap. The other woman took the shaking dog into her arms and petted her reassuringly, saying, "It's all right. You're all right, Tara. No one is going to hurt you." She gave The Father and Anthony an evil look, as if they were the ones who had done something to her dog.

The Mother had been watching all of this, so she gave a great sigh of relief when she saw Suzanne come back to the front desk. The vet tech said, "Wilkinson family, room two please."

"Oh thank goodness," The Mother whispered to herself while gathering up a rather stiff and reluctant Cleopatra. She wanted to get away from that family and their dog before something else happened.

"Well, good morning," Dr. Daisy said as they entered the exam room. "I'm Dr. Daisy, and I don't mind at all if you'd like to call me Dr. D. And who do we have here this morning?" Dr. Daisy had been a veterinarian for a very long time for only one reason: she loved animals, and to her, nothing was more important than making them well and keeping them well. Over the years, she had seen many kinds of animals enter this room, but she stopped for a moment because something was telling her that this was going to be different. She felt for certain that she was going to be taking Jennifer up on that lunch offer.

Suzanne, in her usual robust and businesslike voice, answered, "Doctor, this is the Wilkinson family that Jennifer from The Bowie Animal Shelter called us about earlier. They adopted Anthony and Cleopatra this morning and were so excited to take them home they didn't want to wait for the shelter vet to arrive. So we were happy to help out. It's always a good day when we can be part of bringing a new family together." She handed the doctor the new folders she had made for them and quietly left the room.

All the adults shook hands with each other and said the usual greeting: "Nice to meet you." Jeffrey and Bobby were introduced and told they were very nice and handsome young men.

Then Dr. Daisy said, "Well, let's take a look at this amazing English Mastiff first. You said his name is Anthony?" As if he had been called, Anthony went to her and followed her to the floor scale used for large animals like *BIG DOGS* —dogs that were too big and heavy to be lifted onto the scale built into the exam table. The scale read exactly two hundred pounds. "Wow, you are a big boy, aren't you, Anthony?" She bent down, patted the huge head, and looked into his deep blue-brown eyes. "Yes, what a very good boy you are," she reassured him.

While saying this, she knelt down in front of him and took her stethoscope out of the pocket of her nice new—and clean, thanks to the Saint Bernard triplets—lab coat. Then she placed the earpieces into her ears so she could listen to his chest, but before she touched him, she held the flat round metal part of the scope up to Anthony so he could see it and smell it. Then she said to him in a soothing and calming voice, "Now see this, Anthony? This is nothing to be afraid of. This is nothing that is going to hurt you. I'm going to use this to listen to your chest so I can be sure your heart, lungs, and stomach are good and healthy." The dog sat quietly while she moved the small disk from place to place all over his body.

"Very good, Anthony," she congratulated him. "Everything sounds good and strong. Now I'm going to need you to stand up so that I can feel your insides and be sure everything is in the right place and nothing in there is hurting you. Then I'll take your temperature so I can be sure that you don't have a fever, which could be a sign of an infection. But Anthony..." She paused to rub his head again. "I'm pretty sure that you don't have to worry too much about that. You're a pretty a pretty healthy-looking boy."

Again, as if he had been given a command, Anthony stood up and presented himself for inspection. Dr. Daisy gently poked and prodded him and happily announced that everything was fine. Next she took a flashlight from her pocket and looked first into his eyes and then into his ears. Finally she lifted up his big jowls and lips so that she could see his teeth, which were also perfect. At that moment, Suzanne came back into the room to assist her. "Oh good, Suzanne. You've got perfect timing as usual. Would you please hand me a thermometer so that I can take his temperature?"

While Suzanne looked into the drawer for the thermometer, Dr. Daisy reached for Anthony's rear end, grabbed hold of his tail, and lifted it up.

"You will not touch my Beloved Anthony in such an undignified manner!"

The doctor looked around at the other people in the room, and much to her relief and horror, she could tell they had all heard the voice too. Everyone's eyes frantically searched the faces of the others, looking for someone to confess to playing some kind of joke. Instead she saw that Jeffrey was holding on to his brother's hand and that the younger boy, Bobby, was holding his mother's hand and starting to cry. Finally, with nothing else to explain it, all human eyes turned to The Cat.

Cleopatra had been lying comfortably on The Mother's lap but was comfortable no more. Now she was sitting upright. Her large green eyes somehow seemed even larger and darker. The pupils had become long skinny slits, giving them an almost snakelike appearance. The humans thought they heard her hiss, but later they would talk of it as a soft growl. Dr. Daisy stood up slowly so as not to frighten anyone, meaning Cleopatra. She saw her hands shaking and quickly put them down on the stainless steel surface of the exam table to steady them and herself. Of course, that did not steady her voice when she began to speak.

"W-well, I, er...hmm...think that ma-maybe we can hold off on that temperature for a bit, since he...er...hmm, since he seems to be healthy in all other ways." Her confidence was beginning to come back a little bit. "Of course, I will still need to do his shots..." Her voice trailed off, and again all eyes moved back to Cleopatra, but Dr. Daisy decided to go on anyway, hoping her voice would have the sound of authority that she wanted it to. "Anthony will still need to have rabies and distemper shots for his safety and yours, and I must take his blood in order to check for heartworms and other parasites." The doctor raced through that last part, and when she stopped talking, the entire room was silent.

She let out a very loud sigh of relief that was quickly followed by the sighs of everyone else in the room. Willing to give it one more try, Dr. Daisy asked no one in particular, "Do you think...do you think that it might be possible for me to examine the cat?"

Anthony turned and gave a slight lean, brushed up against the doctor's legs to reassure her that everything would be all right. Then he went over to Cleopatra and ever so gently touched his massive head to hers. "Let the doctor take a look at you, My Lovely. She is very kind and gentle and would never hurt either one of us. She just wants us to be well so that we can go home with our new family."

The Humans watching could see the cat's body lift up and then relax as her head bent down and rubbed against Anthony's. "All right, if you say so, My Dear Husband. I will try."

In one leap she moved from The Mothers' lap onto the exam table, where she sat down. At first both Dr. Daisy and Suzanne took a step backward and sucked in their breath, but all was calm and quiet. The doctor stepped forward, cautiously pulled the stethoscope out of her pocket again, and held it for the cat to see.

This time she spoke even more softly to try to calm and reassure the cat. "This isn't going to hurt you. I'm going to use it to listen to your heart, lungs, and tummy."

Every human in the room held his or her breath as the round disk moved over the cat's body. Not a sound was heard. "So do you think that you might let me feel your tummy so that I can be sure that everything is all right in there?"

The cat stood up and presented herself for further examination. Feeling that she had better get it over with while she still could, Dr. D took out her flashlight and checked Cleopatra's eyes and ears, and she even dared to take a quick look at her teeth. The doctor smiled and nodded at The Family, saying, "Everything looks fine."

Now sometimes people forget things very quickly and simply do what they are used to doing every day. If this had been a normal examination with a normal cat, Suzanne would have assisted Dr. Daisy in taking the cat's temperature. Cats do not usually appreciate having their temperature taken, so Suzanne would normally hold the cat by the skin and hair on the back of its neck with one hand and hold it at the base of its tail with the other hand in order to keep the cat in place. That way the doctor could take the temperature, and no one would get scratched or bitten. Suzanne did this to cats every day, several times a day, so without even thinking about what she was doing or to whom she was doing it, she reached out and grabbed Cleopatra by the scruff of her neck.

Dr. Daisy's voice screamed out, "No! Suzanne, don't."

Then another voice, a more masculine voice, filled the room, saying, "No, My Lovely, do not," but it was too late.

⌒⋀⋙

Wilkinson Family left Dr. Daisy's office in complete silence and continued the ride home the same way. No one knew what to say. No one knew for sure what had happened. The Father looked into the rearview mirror, and yes, his sons were sitting there safe with Anthony between them. They were both petting him without saying a word. The Mother was sitting beside him, and the cat lay contentedly on her lap as she stroked it. Feeling he should not say anything, while at the same time knowing he had to say something, he leaned toward his wife and asked, in what he hoped was a calm whisper, "So do you know what actually happened in there?"

The Mother did not look back at him but kept stroking the cat. "I don't think so. I'm not sure. I know it happened fast, but I just don't know exactly what it was that happened."

"Did you see Suzanne?" The Father was still trying to whisper.

"Well, of course, I saw her. The poor woman. What in the world happened to her? She was almost in her underwear." The Mother stopped petting the cat for a moment and wrapped her arms around herself as if she were suddenly cold. "And that sound. I've only heard a sound like that in the movies, or maybe at the zoo. It sounded like some kind of snarl or even a roar. What kind of animals do they keep in there, and how did it manage to get into the room with us? I'm just glad that the boys are all right."

"Do you think that Suzanne will be OK?"

"I don't know." The Mother was truly worried about the other woman. "As far as I could tell, she didn't seem to actually be hurt. There didn't seem to be a mark on her, but her clothes—"

"What clothes?" The Father found himself blurting out. "The woman hardly had any clothes left on her. Not only were her clothes torn to shreds, but every hair on her head seemed to be standing in a different direction."

The Mother began to stroke the cat on her lap again in an effort to calm herself. "And did you see the look on her face? The poor thing looked almost scared to death, and I could swear that I saw her hair beginning to turn white." She dropped her voice almost to a whisper, only now remembering that The Boys were in the back seat. "And did you see all those long golden-brown hairs all over the place? Where could they have possibly come from?" She paused for a moment, almost afraid of what she wanted to say next. She stopped petting the cat and put her hands down by her sides, safely out of harm's way, before she continued. "You know those hairs, they seemed to be the same color as Cleopatra's."

This time The Father laughed aloud. "That was some kind of joke, wasn't it? Cleopatra? Are you kidding me? I'm not exactly a cat fan or expert, but no house cat could do that to anyone. The woman had to run from the room. And yes, I saw the hairs. I saw the size and thickness of them. No house cat I ever want to meet would have any hairs like that. I don't know what kind of animal got into the room without us seeing it, but it certainly wasn't any house cat." Looking over at Cleopatra, he added, "Not even this rather strange house cat could have done that."

Not knowing what else to say, The Mother just shook her head in wonder as she began to pet Cleopatra again. This time the van began to fill with the soft soothing sound of the cat's purr. Everyone sighed and immediately began to feel better. The Mother turned to look at her husband and then to the back so that she could see Anthony and The Boys.

"You know what, family? We'll just have to call it what it was. It was an unfortunate incident, and we should all promise to never speak of it again. What do you think, guys?"

The Father chimed in with a laugh, "I couldn't agree with you more. That's just the way to handle it."

Then all together they said what they would come to say many times during the years to come: "It was an unfortunate incident, and we promise to never speak of it again."

Coming Home

Even when the trip has only been to the supermarket, arriving home safe and sound always feels so good. So after the morning The Wilkinsons had had, it felt almost like a miracle. No one was surprised when they all almost cheered as the van turned into the driveway of their home.

As the new family of six began to get out of the van, Jeffrey, with his voice full of excitement, said, "So, Dad, are you going to call Uncle Hakeem to let him know that you finally got your BIG DOG?"

With a big grin of pride and satisfaction on his face, The Father was all too happy to respond, "Already have, son. I sent him a quick text while we were leaving the vet's office. He and The Danes should be arriving anytime now. It may have taken me a little longer to get mine, but we'll see who has *THE BIGGEST DOG* now."

Michael Wilkinson and Hakeem Price had been neighbors and best friends since they were five years old. Each of their moms had felt as if she had two sons instead of one because the boys were constantly in and out of each others homes. During summer vacation, the boys ate at whoever s' house they happened to be in during mealtime, and they slept wherever they were at bedtime. During the school year, their mothers did try to keep to a more conventional schedule, but over the weekend, they were known to sneak into each others homes. When their moms put one boy to bed on Friday night, she knew that there was a very good chance that two boys would come down for breakfast on Saturday morning.

Both Michael and Hakeem had enjoyed playing sports all through school but had decided between themselves to never compete against each other for a spot on a team. A toss of a coin had decided that Michael would play football and Hakeem would play basketball. That way they would always be able to be there to cheer for each other. They had attended The University of Maryland together, and while there each had met his future wife, Michelle for Michael and Tina for Hakeem. They were best men at each others weddings and godfathers to each others children. Michael had The Boys, Jeffrey and Bobby, and Hakeem had The Girls, Annalisa and Jessica. All the children called the adults "Aunt" and "Uncle," because in their eyes, that was who they were. The two men were as close as any brothers could be, and over the years, they had worked hard to keep from competing with and against each other. That had worked very well except for one area: DOGS.

As boys they had both wanted and loved dogs. Michael had Samson and Simba, but Hakeem's dad was allergic to dogs, so he had to get his dog fix at his friend's house. This had been OK, but Hakeem had always wanted his own dog. His own *BIG DOG* just like his best friend's, or maybe even *BIGGER*. After they had gotten married, both men felt ready for their own *BIG DOGS* but their wives had stood together, saying no *BIG DOGS* while the children were small.

Hakeem's daughters were older, eleven and eight, so the previous year, his wife, Tina, had given in. Hakeem had raced to *BIG DOG RESCUE* and had come home with not one but *TWO* Great Danes. Sebastian, the tall and handsome black-and-white Harlequin, and his smaller and more delicate black-and-white Boston wife, Julia. Of course, Michael had been happy for his best friend, who then had two BIG DOGS while he had none, but that all changed with the arrival of The Noble Anthony.

The Father and The Boys got Anthony out of the van and headed straight for the backyard to show their BIG DOG his new playground. Since Cleopatra had gone to sleep on her lap, The Mother wrapped her up inside her sweater and carried her into the house. Michelle Wilkinson finally had the cat she had always wanted, and while the men of The Family were outside yelling and jumping with their new best friend, she would be able to sit on the couch for a few minutes and get to know and enjoy hers.

"Well, there you are. I didn't think that you were ever going to get back home. I've been waiting here for you for just hours and hours."

At first the sound of the unexpected voice in the house made The Mother jump off her seat while at the same time holding on to the sleeping ball of Cleopatra inside her sweater. She relaxed as soon as she realized that it was only Auntie Emma-Gene. Yes, it was Auntie Emma-Gene, but how in the world had she gotten into the house?

⌒⁊⋀⊼

Because Michael and Michelle had both grown up in Bowie, they had known Auntie Emma-Gene all their lives. They and everyone else in the town just had no idea of exactly whose aunt she was. All of the people in the town, regardless of their race or ethnicity, seemed to claim her as their own and called her Auntie Emma-Gene, but none of the families had ever been able to figure out exactly how they were related to her. The Father had never cared about who Emma-Gene was related to; he had just thought of her as "a cantaloupe with two little short legs sticking out from under it and a head with a wild mop of brown and gray curly hair sitting on top of it." Even though his wife would shush him for saying it, especially in front of The Boys, inside she had to agree with him.

From Auntie Emma-Gene's sewing machine would come some of the most breathtakingly beautiful bridal gowns, prom gowns, or baptism gowns you would ever want to see, but she always dressed herself in the most horrifyingly huge garish prints that would make grown men beg to be struck blind. Each one of them seemed to be more terrifying than the one before, and each and every one of them was finished off with a dainty and delicate piece of lace at the neck.

Regardless of the color or multiple colors of her dress, it would always be accessorized with what everyone else referred to as THE BEAST, and almost everyone swore that it was alive. Auntie herself simply referred to it as "My Purse." It was a surprise to all who had ever seen this monster that she was always looking for it, because it looked as if it were made from an old piece of red and hot-pink shag carpet from the 1970s. And besides, it was the size of a small bus.

From the depths of THE BEAST, Auntie would pull out grand and glorious things, like the video game that you had been longing for on your birthday and that your parents had said was too expensive if you also expected to have food. Out of THE BEAST would come the most delicate little flower girl's dress all perfectly pressed without a wrinkle in it, or a pan of the world's most delicious bread pudding for the church potluck dinner. It was rumored that at one time, she had actually pulled out a much-longed-for grand piano, complete with the bench and several books of sheet music. Auntie Emma-Gene and THE BEAST were both very well known throughout Bowie and all the surrounding communities.

The Mother looked at the little short round woman, still wondering and asking how she had managed to get into the house while The Family was out. In return, Auntie only said, "Where is she? Where is she? You were supposed to bring her home today, and I've been waiting all this time. I haven't got all day, you know. People think that I do, but I don't. I have a busy schedule too, just like everyone else, you know. It's just that I can't do anything else until I see her."

"Calm down, Auntie, and who in the world are you talking about? You have to see who? And why would she be here?"

The older woman immediately calmed herself, and an air of serenity seemed to come over her as her hands tried to place an ever-loose curl back into her hair. "Why, of course, The Lady Cleopatra, my dear. You and your family were supposed to bring her home today, and I've been waiting for you. There's so much to show you and to teach you, my dear."

At the mention of the cat's name, The Mother felt movement inside her sweater, and then a very sleepy face pushed through the opening. Auntie Emma-Gene squealed in delight and clapped her hands. "Oh, there you are, My Lady. Come to me; it's your Emma-Gene back with you at last."

The Mother stood there and let the cat leave her arms to go to the other woman. She watched as the two rubbed faces together like long-lost friends.

"Oh yes, My Lady, I have made you the most beautiful new things. I think they may be some of my best works ever."

The Mother finally found her voice. "How did you know we were getting a cat today? We didn't even know that we would bring home a cat. And how did you know what her name would be? And furthermore, Auntie, how in the world did you get into the house, because we never ever leave the door unlocked when we're not home?"

"Now, now, my dear, we'll talk about all those things later. Right now we have so much more to go over. Come with me. I've laid everything out in the laundry room. It just seemed like it would be the best place for when you get My Lady dressed in the morning."

The Mother could feel Auntie Emma-Gene's arm around her, guiding her across the kitchen and into the laundry room. She felt certain she should be protesting more, taking a stronger and firmer stand about the unasked-for invasion of her home, but for some reason it just seemed easier to go along with the other woman. The entire laundry room had been transformed. Somehow it seemed to be bigger and brighter, and it may even have been freshly painted. The washing machine and dryer were in their usual places, but all of the typical laundry-room junk and clutter was gone. Even The Boys' backpacks, shoes, and jackets had disappeared from their usual pile on the floor. New cabinets that had never been there before were hanging on the wall above the washer and dryer. Michael had been promising to add some for years, and now, as if out of nowhere, there they were. The Mother opened the doors slowly and carefully, as if she were in someone else's house and the owner would suddenly appear and catch her snooping. Yes, everything she used when doing the laundry was neatly arranged and organized on the shelves. Then, next to it, she realized there was a whole new floor-to-ceiling cabinet. This one went all the way across the wall, and it was divided into five long sections—one for each of them. She could tell because each section had one of their names on it; there was even one for Anthony. How in the world would Auntie Emma-Gene have known about

Anthony, who was supposed to have been Igor, anyway? There was a long section for coats, jackets, sweaters, or ridiculously huge collars and leashes. At the bottom was a shelf where a backpack, briefcase, or handbag could sit, and under that was a bin to hold shoes, boots, and sneakers. Something like this had been on her wish list for years.

"Auntie Emma-Gene, this is just too much." It was all that The Mother could manage to whisper.

"Oh yes, my dear, that's all very nice, but time is short, and this is what I really have to teach you about." She took The Mother by the arm and turned her around to the other side of the room. She still had Cleopatra in her arms, and so she rested the cat on the new counterpoint, which had new cabinets above and below it.

"Now, I think I brought everything—well, at least everything you'll need to get started—and if I have forgotten something, just give me a call, and I'll pop it over to you. So to start with, I put most of The Noble Anthony's things down here," she said, while opening one of the lower cabinet doors. "Being a male, even though he is a very big male, he still doesn't have as many things. So here are his goggles for when he's riding in the car and wants to keep his head out of the window. You know, the wind blowing in their eyes really isn't good for dogs, so you should always protect them with these. It might be a good idea to keep a pair in the car."

Auntie Emma-Gene went on, "Now, in this basket, I put his hats. He doesn't wear them very often, with My Lady riding on his head all the time, but it's a nice change for him once in a while. And here are his boots. There are two kinds, of course, one for rain and one for snow. You can feel free to move these and anything that you want over to the hanging cabinet if that seems to work better for you. Now, even though he's a big boy with a lot of body mass, he still has short hair, so on the very cold winter days, he'll need a coat. I put a couple here, and there is, of course, also a raincoat. I just couldn't resist making it match My Lady's. It's just too cute, isn't it? Now, I didn't think that he would need a rain hat because My Lady's raincoat should come down far enough and protect his head too, but let me know if I was wrong, and I'll whip him up something. Next—"

Only The Mother's tug on her arm stopped Auntie from talking. That and the completely confused look on the young woman's face.

"Auntie, what is going on here? Have you done all this? And if you have, why, not to mention how? How did you even get in here to do all this?" She stood still once again, just looking around the new and oh so very much improved laundry room.

"It's all right, my dear, for you to be a little bit confused now. I know that this is a lot to take in all at one time, but you will, and it will all be just as it should be. Now here I've put all of My Lady's—"

Again The Mother stopped her. "What in the world are all these doll clothes for?"

This time Auntie Emma-Gene's impatience began to show. "Michelle, my dear, you have to pay attention now. You have a lot to learn. These are not doll clothes. These are all for The Lady Cleopatra, and you will dress her in them every day. Now, here are her collars and earrings. You should be able to tell the ones that are for everyday use from those for special occasions. And over here I've put her..." She was pointing to a rack of what looked to be coats or jackets or something.

"I'm not going to dress a cat, Auntie. Not every day and not any time at all. I'm doing good to get myself and The Boys dressed and out the door. I love cats, and I've always wanted a cat, but this has just gone too far." Then her eyes fell on the beautiful gold cape covered in crystals and feathers. Emma-Gene had just barely completed it in time very early this morning. "Oh, how beautiful. This is way too pretty for any doll, and it's so beautifully made."

"Yes, yes, it is, my dear. The Lady Cleopatra will wear this on very special occasions, when she wears the two-part crown called a *Pschent*. The crown represents the unification of Upper and Lower Egypt, and here it is." She pointed to a row of pegs sticking out of a wooden board. It held an entire row of little hats and headpieces, and on one was the red-and-white Pschent, which even had the head of a cobra sticking out of the front. Almost every headpiece had two small holes carefully cut into it—for ears. There was a yellow fisherman's style rain-hat to go with the yellow slicker that The Mother had seen before. And a little straw hat maybe for the summer. This one had to be something for the winter because there was a coat-like thing in the same fabric. The Mother was certain that she was in some kind of daze. Then she felt green eyes staring at her, and she could not keep her hand from reaching out to stroke the brownish-golden fur on Cleopatra's back.

"Everything is so beautiful, and I'm sure that they would look wonderful on you, My Lady. Maybe I could find a little extra time in the morning. The Boys can do more things for themselves now. Auntie has put so much time and work into them, and it would be a shame not to show them off to everyone."

Auntie Emma-Gene looked at Cleopatra, and the two exchanged a knowing smile. "Now one last thing." Auntie opened an upper cabinet door and from the shelf took down a basket. At first The Mother thought that the basket was full of brightly colored Christmas ornaments—very beautiful Christmas ornaments—but Auntie continued, "Now, I brought these for My Lady's…" She paused for a moment. "Let's just say that they are for My Lady's amusement. And they might even help with your dear Michael's safety."

"They look like very fancy and pretty cat toys," The Mother said, while running her hands through them and playing with the ribbons.

"Well, I'm sure that some people might call them that, and, of course, you can too if you wish. I'll just say that they are for My Lady's enjoyment and entertainment, and you will know when to give them to her."

The Mother felt the other woman's arm go around her shoulders and give her a little reassuring hug.

"Relax tonight. Enjoy your pets as the new members of your family that they are. All that you need to know will come to you." Then the soothing tone of the older woman was gone, and the usual whirlwind that was Auntie Emma-Gene had returned.

"Oh my goodness, look at the time," she exclaimed. "And I have so much to do." With a quick bow to the cat, who was still sitting on the counter, she said, "I am so sorry that I have to run, My Lady, but I'll be back soon, and we can have tea and visit." Auntie Emma-Gene looked hurriedly around the room. "Now come, My Dear, where in the world did I leave my purse?"

"I think The BE—no, I mean your purse—is someplace in the family room." A rather dazed and confused Mother followed behind Whirlwind Auntie as everyone usually did.

"Oh yes, here it is." She began digging head first into the enormous carpetbag, which looked as if it could swallow her whole. "Now, I know you and Michael are planning to get The Boys new bikes this spring, so here are their new helmets." Her voice sounded as if she were talking from the depths of some cave, since her head was still buried deep inside THE BEAST. And how did she know about the bikes? The Mother and Michael had never talked to anyone about the new bikes.

"Please try to get the bikes to go with the colors in the helmets. You know how I like for things to be nicely coordinated." She threw the red and hot-pink bag against her orange, green, yellow, and blue plaid dress.

"Now, I must run out back and greet The Noble Anthony before I go, and, of course, I'll have to kiss on The Boys some. I just love the way that those Boys of yours always pretend to hate getting hugs and kisses. It's such a fun game we play together. Oh, and I will try to think of something nice to say to Michael."

Then she stopped, and the cantaloupe of a lady, with the short little legs and the mop of curly hair that would never stay in place, reached up to her "niece" to give her a kiss on the cheek. "I know that it's a lot to take in at one time, my dear, but if you and your family were not The Ones who were needed and who would care for The Noble Anthony and His Lady Cleopatra, then you would have not been chosen." And *poof*—she was gone.

The Mother felt a soft touch against her legs and looked down to see Cleopatra rubbing against her. She bent over and gave the cat a couple of short strokes under her chin. "Well, My Lady," she said with a laugh, "I guess you and I have a lot to learn about each other." She was rewarded with the sound of purring.

⌒⋀⋌

Hakeem, along with Sebastian and Julia, walked around the side of the house and into The Wilkinsons' backyard just in time to see both The

Boys jump onto Anthony's back and to watch *THE BIG DOG* roll over and let them rub his tummy. Michael was sitting in one of the chairs around the table, and Hakeem walked his dogs over to him. "OK, man, I think that you might have won this one because that is *ONE BIG DOG!*"

The Boys heard the familiar voice and came running over, shouting, "Uncle Hakeem, Uncle Hakeem. Come on and meet Anthony."

"Anthony?" their uncle asked The Father as he let The Big Mastiff smell him. Then he rubbed the dog's head in introduction. "I thought that your *BIG DOG* was supposed to be Igor?"

"It was, but he came with Anthony already on his collar, so I decided to go with it because it was a name that he already knew." While the men continued to talk, The Boys searched through their uncle's pockets for the hard candy that they knew they would find. They also discovered a Puppy Cookie for Anthony. Meanwhile, Sebastian and Julia walked over to meet the new *BIG DOG*.

"The Noble Anthony. I am Sebastian, and this is my wife, Julia. We heard that you and The Lady would be arriving today. It is our great pleasure to be one of the first to meet you."

"No, you two are the very first non humans to greet us, and it is my pleasure to meet both of you," answered The Mastiff.

Julia, who was rather shy, gently nudged her husband with her head to remind him. "And My Lady? Is she not here also?"

"Oh yes," Anthony told her with a smile. "My Lady Cleopatra is inside with The Mother. Emma-Gene will be joining them shortly if she is not here already. Come, let us sit here under the oak tree. I am sure that there is much that you can tell me about our new home."

With their father and uncle sitting on the lawn chairs and talking, and with Anthony sitting under the oak tree with the Great Danes, The Boys ran up the street to tell their friends about their wonderful new BIG DOG.

⌒⋙⋘⌒

What a full and busy day this first one with The Family had been. The Boys had thrown anything throw-able for Anthony to catch, retrieve, or play keep-away with. They had ridden him, walked him, and shown him off to the neighbors and anyone else who might have happened to pass by. They had begun to call him Tony or Big Tony, and The Noble One seemed to like it. The Father had dragged the two huge beds he had bought for his BIG DOG from room to room, trying to find the perfect place in the house where he thought Anthony would be the most comfortable. Anthony would eventually put the beds where he wanted them to be, and he picked none of the locations The Father had chosen. The Mother had been in and out of the new laundry room at least twenty times to marvel at all its improvements. The Father, Jeffrey, and Bobby did not seem to notice the changes at all. As much as she tried to ignore all the baskets of small earrings, collars, capes, and coats, she could not stop herself from picking them up, looking at them, and admiring the amazing work that had gone into making them.

There had been a moment of panic around dinnertime because even though The Father had bought enough dog food to keep three dogs of Anthony's size full and happy for at least six months, they realized they had no cat food. On closer inspection, they discovered that Auntie Emma-Gene had thought of everything, and there was a basket full of small cans on a shelf in the laundry room. Sitting beside the basket, in a silver stand of their own so they would never have to touch the floor, were two beautifully etched crystal bowls. They were almost like the one that the big, fluffy white cat on TV ate from. The Mother had looked on this shelf at least a half dozen times before, and she was certain that the bowls, the stand, and the food had not been there. So there was only one thing to do. The Mother whispered, "Thank you, Auntie," and went to feed her beautiful new cat.

After the dinner cleanup, The Family settled comfortably in the family room together to watch a movie. The Boys on the floor with Anthony had very quickly turned Tony (or Big Tony) into their own personal dog couch. Cleopatra had taken up residence on The Mother's lap and had thrilled the woman to no end when The Cat had turned over and presented her tummy to be rubbed. The Father looked across the room at his newly expanded family and found himself to be happy and content. No, his BIG DOG was not named Igor, but he knew that he already loved the big guy no matter what he was called. Of course, there was still this strange cat who had his wife going on about its most wonderful wardrobe, but maybe a cat in the house was not so bad after all. Maybe.

～⁅⁆～

If Anthony was The Father's dog, then Jeffrey and Bobby were Anthony's Boys. The BIG DOG loved them from the moment he first saw them, and he knew he would protect them with his life if he had to. Cleopatra knew that too. It was always like that with her Big Mastiff husband. He would have a strong connection with these boys, especially with Jeffrey, and it would last as long as they were together, but he would be there in times of need for any child. It was Anthony's mission to love and protect His Children, and it was The Lady Cleopatra's mission to love and protect Her Noble Anthony. As The Family sat together watching TV, even Cleopatra had to admit that she enjoyed seeing Jeffrey sitting between Anthony's front legs with his head resting back on the big fur-covered chest and his arms resting on the legs, as if he were lounging in a big brown chair. The Little One, Bobby, had crawled onto the BIG DOG's back and fallen asleep, stretched out on his stomach on his new dog couch. Her Anthony would die for these boys, and for a moment, remembering what had happened so very long ago, Cleopatra felt a wave of sadness come over her.

When it was time for The Boys to go to bed, Anthony, with Cleopatra sitting on his back, waited in the hall because the bathroom was too small for all of them to be in at the same time. The Mother supervised the bathing, the putting on of pajamas, and the brushing of teeth. When they went back to The Boys' bedroom, the two pets, this time with Cleopatra comfortably on Anthony's head, claimed their place between the two beds while The Mother did the bedtime story, prayers, and kisses. Cleopatra loved bedtime stories, but she always wondered why Bastet, the Egyptian Goddess of Cats, or any other cats were never mentioned in the prayers. The Mother wished Her Boys sweet dreams and then called for The Dog and The Cat to come back downstairs with her. Neither of them moved, so The Mother turned off the light and shook her head, knowing that this was an argument she would not win and did not need to. As she went downstairs to rejoin her husband, she had a feeling of peace and happiness because they now had the perfect Family.

The Boys, having said their usual "Good night, Jeffrey," and "Good night, Bobby," burst into a bunch of giggles as they realized that they had not said their good nights to the newest members of The Family. So with lots of laughter, they both said, "Good night, Noble Anthony," and "Good night, Lady Cleopatra," but all the giggles stopped when a voice they had never heard in their house before answered back.

"Boys, there is something that I need to tell you before you go to sleep."

Both Boys immediately sat up straight in their beds and would have screamed if a soft green light had not suddenly filled the room so that they could see the trustworthy face of Anthony looking at them. Even so, seven-year-old Bobby leaped from his bed into the protection of older brother Jeffrey's bed. Safe with his brother, Bobby was then brave enough to ask, "Anthony, was that you? Can you talk?"

This time they could see the unfamiliar but reassuring voice come from Anthony. "Yes, Bobby. There is nothing for you and Jeffrey to be afraid of; it was I speaking to both of you. I can speak, and you can understand me, just as I understand when you speak. It is the same for The Lady Cleopatra." The Lady nodded in agreement.

Now the older (and in his mind wiser) boy, Jeffrey, spoke up. "Wow, this is so cool. Wait till we tell Mom and Dad. They won't believe this. Even better, wait until we tell all the other kids that we have a talking dog!" Then, after a look from green glowing eyes, he quickly added, "Oh, and a cat too."

Before he could finish, Jeffrey could already see Anthony shaking his head no.

"No. You will not tell this to any adult, and the other children will come to know, accept, and understand on their own. Tomorrow we will begin to walk with you to the school bus, and we will do this every day. We will collect the other children in the neighborhood along the way. In the afternoon, we will meet the bus and walk everyone home. By that time, all the children in the county will know, understand, and accept us. When adults are near, we will be able to know each others thoughts just as if we were speaking. Your mother is one of the very few adults who will quietly accept that she can understand us and never question it."

"But, but, but..." The excited younger boy was trying hard to ask something, anything.

"There is no 'but,'" Cleopatra said. "That is how it is and how it always shall be."

Being seven and not yet old enough to know when a subject had been completely closed, Bobby finally blurted out, "But why can you talk? Other dogs and cats can't talk."

"Stop. There will be no more of this." Green eyes now fixed on both boys and froze them in place. "I will tell you this and only this: Many centuries ago, The Noble Anthony made a very great sacrifice in order to protect two human children. As a reward to him for his bravery and sacrifice, The Goddess Bastet gave unto him and all children this gift."

"My Lovely," Anthony whispered to her, "I think that you are frightening The Boys. Though I am sure that you do not mean to."

Cleopatra sighed and rolled her green eyes before speaking again. "I have been told that when given a gift, saying the words 'thank you' is expected. You may say these words now, and then this will never be spoken of again."

Released from their frozen state, both boys quickly said, "Thank you, Anthony. Thank you, Lady Cleopatra."

"Accepted, My Boys. Come, Bobby, and get back into your own bed now."

The little boy was tired, sleepy, and a little unsteady on his feet as he walked the short distance to his bed, but The Big Mastiff was there beside him for support if he should begin to fall. Cleopatra watched from her perch as Anthony carefully pulled the covers over the small boy, who stopped suddenly to hug the neck and kiss the face of his new friend before curling up into his covers.

"Good night, Bobby." There was no response. Anthony could already hear the soft breathing of the little boy's sleep.

When they turned back to the other bed, the older boy was already under the covers, but Jeffrey still reached out, put his arms around The Noble

One's huge neck, and pressed his face against the dog's. "Anthony, I'm so glad that you are My Dog."

"Jeffrey, I am so glad that you are My Boy."

For humans the room had darkened again, but Cleopatra could see the faces of both boys as if it were daylight. She whispered to them through their dreams, "Sleep now, boys. Bastet and The Noble Anthony will guard you as you rest. In the morrow, we will all begin our new life and adventures together."

The dog and cat stayed between the beds in The Boys' room until The Parents came upstairs.

As they looked at their sleeping sons and their new guardians, Michael Wilkinson turned to his wife and said, "Heaven help anyone who makes the mistake of walking into this room uninvited." The Mother pushed at her husband and laughed. Then they walked down the hall to their room.

When all was quiet, Anthony moved down the hall, took his place at the top of the stairs, and lay down. Cleopatra jumped down and took her place between his two huge legs.

"So how does it feel to start again, My Love?" he asked her.

"With you beside me, all feels as it should, My Anthony." She curled herself up into a ball and put her head down. It had been a long day, and she was tired. Anthony put his head down over her. At some time during the night, he would wake her and lead her to the shelf she had chosen in the linen closet. Several times, Anthony would go downstairs and walk through the rooms, sniffing the air and checking for any scents that should not be there. The Big Mastiff paused for a moment, noticing a vaguely familiar but very distant scent that he could not place. He inhaled it again so that he would be certain to remember it. Then he returned to his place at the top of the stairs. He would guard and protect The Parents, His Boys, and His Beloved throughout the night.

The next day, The Mother would remove the towels from what would now be known as Cleopatra's Shelf and replace them with a beautiful red and gold striped bed that Auntie Emma-Gene had made for My Lady. The bed had, of course, just appeared on the kitchen table.

Pronouncement Day

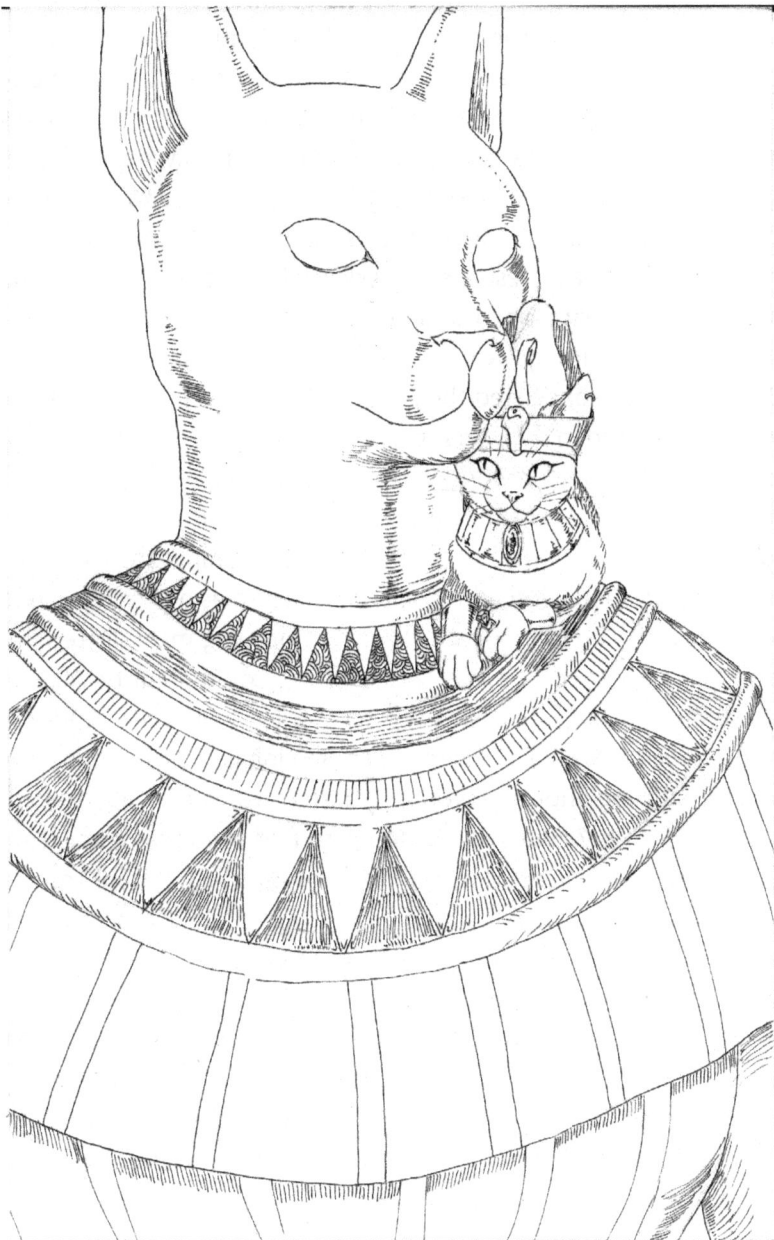

The Temple of Bastet was at its most beautiful in the early morning hours, when the sun was just up and the breeze drifted through the rooms, cooling them and filling them with the rich aromas of the city before the heat of the day arrived. In the main room of the Temple stood a twelve-foot-tall statue of the stately goddess. She was always shown with the body of a woman and the head of a cat. At this Temple, cats were worshiped and loved for being the beautiful, mystical creatures of joy that they are. In the Temple of Bastet, all cats lived in splendor within walls of marble and gold. Soft beds and pillows lay everywhere for them to snuggle on. Servants worked night and day to prepare the richest and most delicious foods for them and to provide for their every want, need, and desire. All the Temple cats were dressed daily in gold and precious jewels, and their coats were brushed with the finest of perfumes. It was considered the greatest of honors to touch one of them or even to be allowed in their presence. This was the world Cleopatra lived in and knew, and this was the world where she belonged.

She stretched out her long, lean body on the softness of the satin pillows and inhaled deeply the scents of the early morning. She could feel the servants moving about in shadows and whispers so as not to disturb her, as well they should. The glorious smells of the morning meal drifted in from the kitchen. If she tried, she was sure that she could identify what would be served this morning. Yes, it had to be chicken lips baked in butter and garlic and served with grilled lizard wings. She inhaled again and knew that there would also be another favorite—roasted worm toes in savory herbs. But wait. Could it be? Had they managed to find the most wonderful dish of all? Fried hummingbird lips with fresh honey to dip them in! Truly, it was going to be a very good day. It would be a very good day because it was also Pronouncement Day.

During every third full moon, at the change of the seasons, all the kittens that had been born throughout the city and surrounding lands were brought to the Temple of Bastet to be presented and blessed by her and her human handmaidens. There was music, dancing, and food for all, for Bastet was also the goddess of joy. The kittens were bathed and then brushed with scented oils until their coats glistened. Then they would be presented to

Bastet by handmaidens, who would share with the crowd each kitten's future and, if need be, change the kitten's name to something more suited to the destiny that had been foretold for it.

"My Lady, My Lady, come now. It's time to get up." Cleopatra woke reluctantly from her red and gold bed on the linen-closet shelf. Something very large, soft, and somewhat wet was pushing against her body. She reached out and wrapped her arms around it and rubbed her head against the huge muzzle of Her Beloved.

"Not now, Anthony. I was having—"

He gently interrupted her. "I know, My Dear. You were having the dream about breakfast in The Temple of Bastet."

"How did you know?" she asked in wonder and just a little bit of annoyance that he should know her so well, while at the same time a giant tongue was licking her face. "Stop that!" she said, although she did not push him away. In fact, she reached up with her arms and held the great Mastiff head of The Noble Anthony between her paws. Gently she rubbed her small head against his massive one, being sure to touch the side of her mouth against his, to mark him as her own.

"I can always tell when you are having that dream because even in your sleep, you are smiling."

"Well, good morning anyway, My Handsome One," she whispered in her soft Abyssinian purr.

"And good morning to you, My Beloved One. Come now, you sleepy head. I did not want to wake you this early, but it is a special day, and you have to get ready. The Mother is waiting to give you breakfast and assist you in dressing. So come now. We have a lot to do, and we cannot be late for the school bus."

She stood up on her shelf in the linen closet and stretched out the morning kinks. "Oh, Anthony, not more of that foul-smelling whatever it is in those cans. I refuse to call it food, is not fit even to feed to the beasts."

"I know, My Beloved, but unfortunately hummingbird lips will not be served in the laundry room this morning. You know how The Mother worries about you. You eat my food, but The Mother maintains that even though my food is perfect for a big dog like me, it does not have the vitamins that you need to be your most beautiful self."

Cleopatra could not deny Her Anthony anything. "All right. I'll try." But the cat showed no interest at all in moving. In fact she lay her head on top of his big nose and wrapped her arms around his mouth to stop him from talking. "Breakfast. The Mother is a gentle woman, but she has no idea of what a good breakfast is." Finally, reluctantly, she said, "Give me a kiss so that we can get this over with. Wait." She sat up suddenly. "You said that today is a special day. What special day is it?"

"You have talked about almost nothing else for weeks. I cannot believe; now that it is finally here, you have forgotten about Pronouncement Day. Please do not let Sniffer know you forgot. I only got him to agree to this because I told him it was important to you. He would not be happy if he thought you had forgotten about it."

"Pronouncement Day! How could I have forgotten?" She began to quickly lick both her paws and brush them over her face, smoothing back her long whiskers and fur. "How do I look?"

"You look lovely as usual, My Beloved, but no kiss before we go?"

"All right, but just one." Obediently The Noble Anthony gave her a loving kiss between her ears, causing his big jowls to momentarily cover most of her head.

Once she could see again, she smiled up at her husband's big handsome face. "Yes, now we must go, My Love. We do not want The Father to become upset and repeat that unfortunate incident we had at the library."

She jumped from her shelf onto his back for the ride down to the kitchen.

The entire universe knew that Cleopatra loved kittens, and there were even rumors that she actually played with them from time to time. Some went as far as to say that she had once been a kitten herself, but no one truly believed that. Whenever a new kitten arrived in the neighborhood, she would be there to meet it. Soon after, the word would go out for the date and time of the kitten's Pronouncement Day. On that day, Cleopatra would, in the name of The Goddess Bastet, bless the kitten, tell of its future, and if need be, change its name. All the children would be there, and so would any parents who could. It was a very exciting day.

Downstairs, the morning activities were going on as usual. The Father was at the far end of the kitchen table, trying to read a few more lines of his newspaper and have one or two more swallows of his coffee before leaving for his office. The Boys were shoving down the last couple of spoonfuls of their cereal and fruit while debating what new name might be given to the kitten who was now called Alexx. Meanwhile, The Mother was in the laundry room, impatiently waiting for Cleopatra to arrive.

"Oh, Anthony, there you are. Thank you so much. I knew that you would be able to get her. This would be the one morning that I have an early meeting." Turning her attention now to the cat sitting on the dog's back, The Mother said, "If you will, My Lady, I know you don't have much time for breakfast, but please try to eat something. You can have more when you get back." She carefully, with one hand supporting her chest and the other hand supporting her hind legs, lifted the cat from Anthony's back and placed her on the counter in front of the stand holding the crystal bowl filled with *Le Kit-tay Cat Food.*

Cleopatra turned to Anthony, who stood beside her on the floor. "So this was the horrible stench that greeted me as we came down the stairs."

"Just try a little of it, My Dear. You know how The Mother worries about you. She tries so hard to find something that you might like. Try just a little?"

The Mother watched as Cleopatra, hardly looking at the food in the bowl, made scratching motions back and forth around it with her paw, trying to bury the foul smell with some invisible covering. The Mother had seen this many times before. Michelle Wilkinson sighed, thinking she would now have to try yet another brand.

"OK, My Lady, I give up. They always sound better in the store, but I suppose that I should have known that something called *Bar-B-Qued Turnip Surprise* was not going to be all that great. I know it's not what you were used to in The Temple—and I don't even know what in the world they gave you in that Temple—but I promise you, this is the best that I can do." This time, showing her frustration, she blurted out, "You know it's also not nice to actually try to bury the food that someone offers you." The Mother sighed, knowing that it was time to give in and give up. "You were right anyway. It does smell horrible. Will you once again please forgive me?" She just had to laugh. "You can have some of Anthony's food when you get back. Now let's get you dressed."

From the long full rack of what she had once called "doll clothes," The Mother chose the long gold cape that was covered in multicolored crystals and feathers. She carefully arranged it around the cat's slight shoulders and then fastened the ties into a bow to hold it securely in place.

"So what do you think will be best today? The large red collar, which has always been my favorite, or the green one, which will actually go better with your eyes and ring?"

The Mother held the two sparkling necklaces in front of the cat, who lifted her paw and touched the green one to show her acceptance of it. "You are right, My Lady, as always. The green will be so much better."

The Mother lifted this over Cleopatra's head so it would rest on her chest and wrap around her shoulders. The necklace would tie in the back. Now for her headpiece. Even though Auntie Emma-Gene had originally made the crown of Upper and Lower Egypt, called a Pschent, with a white upper cone and a red band, yesterday she had left a new one on the kitchen table with a note that read:

> I've been thinking about it, and I feel that this Pschent with the white cone and gold band will look better with My Lady's gold cape. You know how I like things to be nicely coordinated. Will try to make it to the Pronouncement if I can.
> Love, Auntie

The Mother picked up the delicate little cap and turned it around in her hands for a moment, once again admiring Auntie Emma-Gene's exquisite work. It wasn't until she felt a paw on her arm that she said, "Oh yes, My

Lady, you are right. I can't stand here in a daze. We all have to get moving this morning. Now hold your head up just like this." Very slowly she guided the little crown straight down so that it slid over Cleopatra's ears perfectly. "There, you look elegant. Come, Anthony, now it's your turn."

Anthony did not usually wear anything on Pronouncement Day. He had let The Mother know that His Lady Cleopatra was the only ornamentation he needed. Still, The Mother had been thinking maybe he should have some-thing, so it did not come as much of a surprise when she went to the kitchen this morning and found a new box, with another note from Auntie Emma-Gene. The note read:

> Dear One,
>   This is a Nemes headdress. You may have seen pictures of the Egyptian King Tut wearing a blue and gold one. Our Noble Anthony is not a king, but I thought that one in the gold like My Lady's cape would be nice. Once again, you know how I like things to coordinate.
> Love, Auntie

The Mother had looked around the kitchen, expecting to see if not Auntie herself, then at least THE BEAST of a purse that she carried around all the time. Of course, there had not been any sign of either one, so she only shrugged her shoulders and opened the box. The Nemes was spectacular. She felt for sure that it was much more beautiful than the pictures she had seen of King Tut's headdress. It was also gigantic and could easily have been worn by any kind of giant, jolly or not, so, of course, it should fit Anthony perfectly.

"Come on, Anthony; let's get you even more good looking than you usu-ally are." She lifted the headpiece and let the leather band slide down over the dog's forehead. The carving of the single cobra stood out from the band and sat perfectly between his eyes. The billowy fabric covered his ears, but the side panels lay down over his shoulders, giving him the look of ears lon-ger than Sniffer's the Bloodhound.

"Anthony, I think Auntie Emma-Gene has done it again, because you do look amazingly handsome." She bent down, took the BIG DOG's face into her hands, and gave him a big kiss right on the top of his nose. "I love you, Anthony."

"And I love you, Mother of My Boys," she heard him reply. Michelle Wilkinson was no longer surprised at hearing the thoughts of the dog and cat in her head. In fact, she found it to feel very normal and comfortable. She just didn't bother to mention it to her husband. She turned to the waiting cat.

"Shall I place you on Anthony now, My Lady?" The cat nodded, and The Mother lifted her ever so carefully. Anthony sat up even taller as he prepared himself to receive His Lovely. The cape had been cut perfectly. The front just kissed the tops of her feet but still showed her gold leg bands and her ring, and the rear softly draped down the back of Anthony's head, blending perfectly with his new Nemes headpiece.

"Stunning. You both look absolutely stunning. Now we have to go."

As they walked back into the kitchen, Michael Wilkinson, who had heard all of this from where he sat in the kitchen, shook his head in disbelief. He loved his wife, but this was just too much. A cat whom you had to ask to forgive you? A cat who had a better wardrobe—custom-made—than most people? A cat who rode around on a dog's head? No one else on the planet had pets like these. This was going to be another humiliating day. After all, some of the people there might know him, and it seemed that EVERYONE knew Cleopatra.

"I hope no one from my office sees this," he said aloud to no one in particular before hiding himself in the paper again.

The Boys were waiting at the front door with their backpacks all ready to go. Bobby opened the door and bowed slightly as Anthony and The Lady walked through. Most of the children whom Anthony usually collected in the morning to escort to the school bus stop were already waiting on the porch, and the last few were running toward the house. The Noble Anthony paused for a moment to let them catch up and also to give all the others a chance to admire His Lovely Lady. It had been a while since the last Pronouncement Day. Of course, everyone had seen Cleopatra in her formal robes before; still the children could not hold back their responses: "Oh wow" and, Cleopatra's personal favorite, "She's beautiful."

Today they also had to add, "Wow, look at Big Tony," and "Boy, he really is The Noble Anthony today."

Anthony took in a deep breath. By inhaling the scents of all the children, he could take roll call as teachers do in school. His wonderful dog nose could tell in an instant if everyone was there. He could also tell the scents of the parents and their relationship to each child, any older brothers and sisters who may have stopped by on the way to their bus stop, or even any of the usual delivery people in the neighborhood. With this one breath, he could also tell if there was anyone new among them. That was why Cleopatra could feel his body stiffen beneath her feet and feel his head move slowly as his eyes scanned the small crowd, looking for the source of the new scent. She whispered to him so that the children could not hear, "What is it, My Love? What do you sense?"

"I am not sure. It may be nothing. I think that there are two new men someplace near."

"Could they be here for someone else? You know, like when Miles, the regular UPS man, went on vacation and that very nice Bruce took his place."

"Yes, I am sure that it is something like that, but during our first night with The Family, when I did my walk through the house, I noticed their scent. Why would a UPS man be in the neighborhood in the middle of the night? Their scent is somehow familiar, and yet I cannot remember why or from where. I only know that there is something about their scent that bothers me a great deal."

The Big Mastiff suddenly realized that there were many pairs of eyes looking at him, waiting for him to move forward. "Regardless, My Lovely. We had better get going to Sniffer's house. I am certain that it will come to me eventually."

As Anthony began to move, it looked as if the entire neighborhood were moving with him. They formed quite a parade, with the dog and cat leading the way and numerous children and adults following.

Sniffer the Bloodhound had lived with the Taylor family for five years. The parents took good care of him, and he loved his two little girls, Lisa and

Linda, with all his big Bloodhound heart. He even loved them when they painted his toenails yellow and put pink ribbons around his long hound ears and tied them into lovely bows. He would endure any embarrassment that made His Girls giggle, laugh, hug, and kiss him and love him more. Sniffer had considered the family to be perfect and complete, and he had seen no reason for any additions to it, except maybe if it had been another little girl to love him, but the new member of the family had not been another little girl. It had been a boy, and to make matters worse, it had been a boy KITTEN.

Sniffer knew there were many dogs who lived with cats and did not seem to mind it at all, but he did not know how they managed to do it, with that cat smell and all. Maybe Anthony could tell him. Maybe the big Mastiff could give him an idea or two on how to manage living with a cat, of all things. The Bloodhound looked up the street, and from his seat on the porch of his house, he could see the procession getting closer. What a relief. All of this would soon be over. As much as he loved and would die for the two little girls beside him, they might have gone too far this time. This time not only had his toenails been painted blue and blue bows been put on his ears, because the kitten was a boy, but he had to sit here on the porch with the handle of a basket in his mouth, holding the sleeping kitten. This really was too much, but just then his girl Linda leaned over, gave him a big kiss on his nose, and patted his head while telling him what a good boy he was. Well, maybe he could sit here for a while longer. At least there were no ribbons on his tail this time.

Anthony, Cleopatra, all the children, and all the parents arrived at the Taylor house and stopped in front of Sniffer, his two girls, and the sleeping kitten, Alexx, in the basket. Anthony spoke. "Sniffer, The Lady Cleopatra is here, in the presence of all who are gathered with us today, to bless The Kitten Alexx and to share his future. Do you accept this?"

"Yes, Noble Anthony, I do accept this." Sniffer immediately wondered why he had said that. He was only here because his Girls had offered him puppy treats and tummy rubs if he was a good boy and did what they asked. Whether he had wanted to say the words or not, Sniffer had still said them, and so Anthony lay down in front of him and rested his head between his legs onto the concrete. The Girls nudged at Sniffer to put the basket down on the ground in front of The Mastiff. Cleopatra walked down the front of Anthony's face and over his nose to her place beside the basket and looked at the still-sleeping kitten inside.

"Oh, he is SO handsome," she said, her voice dripping with praise and pleasure.

At eight weeks old, Alexx was just about as cute as he was ever going to be. His long coat was all fluffed out around him, making him look like a little fluff ball with a pink nose and ears. A white mask began at the top of his nose, spread out over his muzzle, went down his throat, and spread out over his tummy, which was just waiting to be rubbed. When he turned a little bit, Cleopatra could see his black and gray "tiger" stripes. Cleopatra licked one of her paws and then softly and lovingly swiped it over the kitten's face, smoothing out his whiskers and gently laying down his ears. As she did this, she began to purr the sacred purr of Bastet, The Goddess of All Cats. She bent her head down into the basket, closed her eyes, and smiled while rubbing her head and the side of her mouth against the kitten's, marking him as her own. For a moment she seemed to forget where she was. She said, "Oh, Anthony, he smells so wonderful. Nothing is better than New-Kitten Smell."

Still smiling, she turned toward Anthony and climbed back onto his head. Once she was in place, he sat up and turned toward the crowd so that she could speak to all who could hear and understand her—which meant all the children.

"Goddess Bastet, protector of all cats and of all whom cats love, this day I ask you to pour your many blessings on to this kitten, today known as Alexx."

Suddenly, whispers filled the air from the crowd of children, as they told their parents what was happening, because Cleopatra's words meant that the kitten's name was going to be changed.

"This kitten will become the best and lifelong friend of his companion, Sniffer. They will laugh, play, and have many wonderful and great adventures together. They will love and protect each other and Their Human Family. Because of this, The Kitten will no longer be known as Alexx. From this day forward, this kitten will become the cat that will be known as The Great Alexander. This name is given to him because of the many great and wonderful things that will happen to him and to all who love him."

The crowd cheered and applauded. Anthony beamed with his pride in His Lovely Lady, and Cleopatra beamed with pride in herself. It was a wonderful day, and all was as it should be.

Then Sniffer spoke. "So tell me, Anthony, people tell me that you've been with The Lady here a very long time. Some even say that you two have been together for centuries and that this cat is your wife. I don't really care about all that. To each his own, I always say, but there is something that I'm going to need to know if I'm going to be having all these big and great adventures The Lady was going on about. I need to know how you deal with the smell?"

A dark cloud of quiet fell over children and parents alike, even though the parents were not sure why. The quiet was like the quiet that would have existed if laughter and speech had never been invented. Eyes went back and forth as the people looked at each other, not being sure of what they had heard (or for the parents, of what their children were telling them). So they all looked at Cleopatra, whose smile had disappeared, whose joyful purring had stopped, whose eyes had turned to snake slits, and whose height seemed to have grown three times as tall as she used to be.

The Noble Anthony tried to speak, but at first nothing came out. Then he tried again. "Sir, um, Sniffer, what smell could you possibly be talking about?

"Now, this would have been a good time for Sniffer to say something like, "Smell? Did I say 'smell'? Silly me, I meant to say 'kisses.' How do you deal with all the kisses that you get from your cat?" But Sniffer did not say anything about kisses. What the Bloodhound did say was "You know the smell that I'm talking about, Anthony. THE CAT SMELL. You have to tell me how in the world you deal with that cat smell because I don't think that I'm going to be able to handle it. The little guy is only a baby, and I can hardly stand it. I can't imagine what it's going to be like when he's all grown up."

"ENOUGH OF THIS OUTRAGE!"

No one would ever have to ask who had said that. Cleopatra had jumped down from Anthony's head and was now sitting on the concrete driveway, with her green eyes staring into Sniffer's. Children who were with a parent or near any adult turned to them and tried to hide their faces in a pant leg, or the side of a sweater, or anything that would hide what was sure to come. The Adults, who had not actually heard anything, took a step backward and wondered if this might not be a good time to leave with their children, even if they were not sure why.

Anthony used his foot to pull the basket with the still-sleeping kitten closer to him for protection while at the same time trying to move his body a little more in between Sniffer and His Lady. He knew that this would not protect the other dog, but still he felt the need to at least try.

"How dare you? How dare you, you whimpering, mange-infested son of a jackal!"

Sniffer felt his legs give way as he whimpered and cowered with his head down.

"You are not worthy of being the caretaker of this cat and his human family. Since you find the smell of cats to be so offensive to you, then maybe the smell of mud, swamps, and decaying plants would be better suited to you. Since you have proven yourself to be unworthy of living in the service of a cat, then maybe the rest of your life would be better spent as A TOAD!"

A gasp of surprise and horror flowed from the children to the parents. Then the voice of The Noble Anthony broke through. In a tone of command that Jeffrey and Bobby had never heard before and that only they could hear, Anthony said to His Boys, "Quick, take all the others to the bus stop. I promise you Sniffer will not be harmed. By the time I come to get you this afternoon, all the others will have forgotten this part ever happened. Go now."

Before Jeffrey and Bobby could think of anything to say, they watched in shock, surprise, and horror as The Big Mastiff grabbed His Lovely Lady by the back of the neck, picked her up with his mouth, and ran down the street back toward their house.

"Anthony, what are you doing? Put me down! Put me down this instant!"

"I will, My Lovely, as soon as I have you safely home." The reply was muffled, spoken through a mouth full of fur and jeweled collar.

Anthony did not slow down until he reached the side door of their home, which entered into the laundry room. Auntie Emma-Gene had thoughtfully provided a door designed to let a cat or a dog go in or out on its own. There was also a panel that could be slid into place so that the door could be completely locked. It was called a Puppy Door, but the name sounded ridiculous given the size that was needed for The Noble Mastiff. Still holding her in his mouth in a gentle but highly undignified manner, Anthony carefully pushed through the door and placed the ruffled and disheveled cat on the floor. His Nemes head dress caught on the flap of the Puppy Door and fell onto the floor, in a pile, but The Mastiff paid no attention to it. Finally he sat down and waited, not saying a word.

"How could you? How could you do this to me? You picked me up as if I were a sack of cow dung and carried me through the streets for all to see." The cat paced back and forth, and as she spoke her tail twitched and crackled like a whip under her gold robe. The Pschent had fallen off her head as they came through the door, and it was clanging as it rolled on the floor. "How could you do this after that creature said those horrible things about me? Did you not hear what he said to me? He said that I *SMELL*. Did you not hear that part? That horrible creature said that I, Cleopatra, descendant of The Goddess Bastet herself, *SMELL!*"

The entire house shook.

"Well, My Beloved, you do smell, and I could not let you turn Sniffer into a toad because he spoke the truth." The Mastiff's voice was soft but, at the same time, commanding and unafraid.

This time houses for two blocks over shook. Several people actually called the local news stations to ask if an earthquake had been reported.

Cleopatra stopped in her tracks. She stood up on her hind legs and rested her paws on the big dog's muzzle so that she could look directly into his soulful blue-brown eyes. "My Anthony, you have been my love and my husband through all the centuries, and I will now ask you to explain what you could possibly mean by those words." She let go of him and sat down in front of him, waiting for his answer.

"My Beloved, you do smell, and to me, it is the most glorious of smells. To a dog, almost all things have a scent or smell. It is even more so for a dog like Sniffer. He is a Bloodhound. Humans have bred him to smell and to find things. He can smell things that even I cannot. Most smells are wonderful, like those of The Mother. She smells of cooking food, the garden, the people she knows at work, dog cookies and boy cookies, love, and The Boys themselves. She also smells of her love for The Father, and she smells of caring for all of us.

"My Boys smell of me since we play together all the time. Of course, they also smell of grass and sweat and then of learning, growing, and sharing with the other children, and they smell of the love and respect they learn for all things. Naturally they also smell of Their Parents and all the things that surround them. All these things are part of the scent or smell that makes them who they are.

"You even said yourself the kitten had the sweet smell of new life. And you, My Darling..." The Big Dog's voice softened as he lay down so that he would be on the same level with her. He brushed her head with the side of his to remind her that he was her own. "You, My Darling, My Love, and My Most Glorious Wife, have the most wondrous scent of all. Because of your scent, I could find you and come to your rescue even if you were ten miles away and covered in those horrible stink bugs. You smell of the incense of The Temple. You smell of the love that we have shared with each other over hundreds of years. You smell of the people whom we have met and loved and who have loved and cared for us over our many adventures together. You smell of the children we have helped to raise to adulthood, and you smell of every kitten that you have blessed. You smell of the very first tear that you ever cried and of the last time that you allowed yourself to laugh. You smell of The Lady Emma-Gene, who has served us both well and for so long. Best of all, you smell of me and of the great love that I have had for you through all of time. For all beings, their scent or smell is part of who they are, and it is a wonderful thing."

Cleopatra looked deep into the beautiful, sad eyes of her husband and remembered why she had loved him so through all the ages. Her eyes fought back tears of joy and admiration. This noble creature was her true love. She cleared her throat and held up her head. "Oh yes. All of that. I understand now what he might have meant. For a dog like Sniffer, even a good smell can get to be, maybe a bit too much. Too strong or too intense."

"And, My Darling, let me also say that you cannot turn someone into a toad just because you do not like what they have said about you. It is not nice; they will not like it, and they will not like you any better."

"But—" The cat was ready to begin her protest all over again. After all, SHE was The Lady Cleopatra.

"No, My Lovely, you cannot. It would displease and disappoint me so very much. Let us not speak of this for a while. Come, let us go into the sunroom. I feel that we could both use some rest before Our Boys and the other children return, but first I will help you disrobe."

It was not easy for THE BIG DOG to grab hold of the tiny lace that made part of the bow that held Cleopatra's jeweled collar in place, especially since he had to do it with his teeth. He was working with Cleopatra's small head and an even smaller bow. Sometimes her head would get lost in his mouth, but after a few tries, he did manage to get it loose. The cape was much harder because it had been tied in the front under her chin, but after she jumped up onto the counter, he was able to reach underneath, grab the end from around her neck, and pull it, and the cape slipped off her shoulders. She was free from her robes, but her head and shoulders were a wet slobbery mess. Having a husband with no fingers or thumbs and a head that was larger than her entire body, did at times have its drawbacks.

She quickly licked one of her front paws and drew it over her whiskers a couple of times, but her paw was then wetter than when she had begun. This would take forever, so there was only one thing to be done. She sat very still, closed her eyes, and purred the special purr of joy, happiness, and love. In less than a minute, each and every golden-brown hair had dried and laid itself down perfectly. Anthony looked at her admiringly. "It always fascinates me when you do that. How do you manage to go from being, I say with all love, a wet mess to being your most beautiful and serene self in a matter of seconds?"

"I do not know. Must be magic." She winked a green eye at him. She walked beside Her Love into the sunroom that had been built onto the back of the house. It was her favorite room, and Anthony lay down and rested his head on the floor in the perfect sunny spot. She jumped up onto his back and then walked to his head. She let her legs spread out underneath her and wrapped herself lovingly around Her Anthony's giant head. Giving it one last try, she asked, "And the toad part. You are sure about the entire not changing into a toad part?"

"Yes, My Lady. I am very sure about the toad part. When we go to meet the children this afternoon, we can stop at his house, and you can apologize to Sniffer then."

"What? I have to apologize to Sniffer too?" She quickly sat up. This whole thing just seemed to be getting worse and worse. "Is not the fact that he will not be living out his life in the swamp and the mud or on a lily pad enough?"

"My Lovely—"

"All right. If I have to do this, it is better that it be done when it is just the three of us. The humiliation of this day will just not ever end. I never had to apologize when we lived in The Temple." She settled herself back down onto Anthony's head and pouted.

The Big Dog took a deep breath in, and as he let it out, his whole body relaxed onto the floor. "I know, but we do not live in The Temple anymore. Now purr us to sleep and let us rest. We have both had quite a morning."

Resigned to her fate, The Lady could only say, "I love you, My Anthony."

"And I love you, My Lovely."

⌒ᛉ⌒

In the afternoon, the two began the walk up the street to meet the school bus. As they approached the Taylor house, Cleopatra could see Sniffer sitting on the porch with the kitten's basket beside him. In her heart, Cleopatra had been hoping The Bloodhound's Family had taken him to the vet or some other unpleasant place so that she would not have to go through with this, but it seemed that Bastet was not smiling on either one of them that day. It did not help when Anthony said, "Oh yes, there he is." Before she was ready, she and Anthony were standing in front of Sniffer and The Great Alexander. Anthony had watched the other dog stand and then step backward in an attempt to put more space between himself and The Cat after what had happened that morning. So The Mastiff spoke up to try to put Sniffer at ease. "Good day, Sniffer. We have come here this afternoon so The Lady Cleopatra might speak to you."

"Sniffer," Cleopatra tried to begin. Then she stopped and started again. "Sniffer, I have been told by The Noble Anthony that I owe you an apology. Since we all know Anthony speaks only the truth, then it must be so. He has also explained to me that because a dog's sense of smell, and a Bloodhound's especially, is so strongly developed, there are times when even a pleasant odor or smell can become overwhelming. That would, of course, make the scent unpleasant. So, I was wrong to think that you were insulting me when I did not have all the facts to know that for certain. Also..." This was the part that she hated the most. "Also, I should not have threatened to turn you into a toad because you said something about me that I did not like or feel was true. You have a right to your own opinions, be they right or wrong, and so, Sniffer, I ask for your forgiveness in this matter."

Sniffer was obviously feeling better and more secure after Cleopatra's speech. He walked right up to them and said, "Well, Lady Cleopatra, I have to say that I was a bit frightened there at the beginning when you arrived. I've never much liked toads, but as you can see, no harm was done—in the toad-turning part, that is—so I guess I can say 'apology accepted.'"

Anthony sighed a bit and was preparing to continue their walk when Sniffer began to speak again.

"You know, I don't know if it has anything to do with the words that you said over him this morning, but the little guy..." He pointed his head toward the basket, which the little one was trying to climb out of. "He's just not smelling all that bad to me anymore."

Anthony could feel the tips of Cleopatra's claws beginning to extend until they just barely touched his skin. "My Lady," he said, trying to calm and reassure her.

"I am happy to hear that we have both become so educated to new things today." Anthony breathed another sigh of relief, until Cleopatra spoke again. "Oh, and it has come to my understanding that you like to sleep on your back with your rather long, even for a Bloodhound, ears spread out all over the floor."

Sniffer took one or two steps back again. No one but his family knew about that. How could this cat know? "Well, yes, My Lady, sometimes I do. No one has ever seen any harm in it. My Humans say that I'm a good boy, and My Girls like to rub my tummy when I lay that way. I kind of like that part myself."

"No, there is no harm in your sleeping on your back—especially since The Great Alexander likes to sleep on one of your outstretched ears or curl up beneath one of them. I just thought that I should let you know that, in the future, that might become a little more difficult to manage."

Cleopatra smiled a secret cat smile and flicked her tail to let Anthony know that she was ready to leave.

"My Dear One, why did you say—"

Smiling to herself, she softly interrupted him. "Oh, it was nothing, My Beloved. I just thought he should begin to prepare himself for the future. That is all."

The children's walk back home from the bus stop had been much quieter than usual. That is, until they arrived at the Taylor house. Though none of the children except Jeffrey and Bobby could remember exactly what had happened there that morning, they still looked relieved when everyone could see that Sniffer was still a Bloodhound. It was Bobby, the youngest of the group and one who had full memory of what had happened, who could not hide his excitement. "Look, look! Sniffer is still a dog and not a toad.'"

"Of course, Little One." The cat purred. "All is as it should be."

The New Girl in Town

Because the city of Bowie is close to the nation's capital, Washington, DC, there are several military bases not very far away, and a lot of military families live there. Military families have to go where they are needed, which means that they often have to move, a lot. That was what had brought the Nelsons—with their daughter, Gwen—to Bowie. Both of Gwen's parents were in the Air Force, and this was the perfect location to allow them to get to their bases quickly.

Gwen was nine years old, and the family had moved four times since she was born. This meant that Gwen had attended four different schools in four different states. She also had to make friends and then leave them four different times. Most of the time, Gwen liked being part of a Military Family. She was very proud that both her parents had chosen to serve their country. In the past, most of the children she had gone to school with had attended the same school all their lives, but she got to say things like, "When I went to school in Seattle, we did reading groups like this," or "When I lived in Tampa, we always had to be on the lookout for alligators when we played outside," or "When we lived in Texas, my school was on the base, so I could ride my bike to school every day." Yes, sometimes it was nice to be a little special and different. Sometimes it was nice to have different things to talk about, and sometimes it was not.

This time when the family moved, the school year had already started. Some of the children who lived near each other had done things together over the summer, like Vacation Bible School, Boy Scouts, or Girl Scouts, or had gone to day camp together. Others had already reconnected with the friends whom they had not seen all summer. Still others had discovered new friends they had been going to school with but had never noticed before. It was hard to be the new kid in a school where it felt as if all the friendships had already been made and where there did not seem to be anyone left for you.

Mrs. Nelson had been worried about her daughter's ability to make new friends, so she was not only very surprised but also very pleased when she opened the front door to walk her daughter to the school bus stop for her first day and found a group of children waiting for her at the foot of the driveway. A group of children in the company of an extremely large dog who had a very strange cat wearing jewelry sitting on top of his head.

One of the boys walked up to her and said, "Good morning, Mrs. Nelson. My name is Jeffrey Wilkinson, and this is my younger brother, Bobby." The boy was very nice and polite, but given the time she had spent getting un-packed, trying to find her way to her new job, and learning all her new re-sponsibilities at work, Mrs. Nelson had not had a chance to meet any of their neighbors. So how did Jeffrey know their name was Nelson?

The boy went on, "You're welcome to come to the bus stop with us if you want to, but my dog, Anthony, and The Lady Cleopatra will be here every morning while school is in session to walk Gwen to the bus stop. Then we'll bring her home in the afternoon. Anthony said to tell you that Gwen will always be safe with us."

"Well, thank you, Jeffrey. That's very kind of you and all the others." But what Mrs. Nelson was thinking was "How does he know my daughter's name?" and "THE DOG said that she would be safe?"

"But you know, Jeffrey, since this is Gwen's first day, I think that I'll just walk along with all of you, if you don't mind." As they walked along with the dog and the cat leading the way, Mrs. Nelson listened to the other chil-dren and realized that they all seemed to know her daughter's name. Some were speculating on who her teacher might be. Well, at least they did not already know that. Someone else promised to look for her at lunchtime. A car went by, and a hand waved out the window while a voice shouted out, "Hey, Anthony. Hey, Miss C." So other people knew this strange cat and dog too. As they walked, they were joined by a couple of other children, and she heard, "You must be Gwen. My name is Hanna. I hope we can be friends."

They stopped at the corner because they had to cross the street. Mrs. Nelson was thinking there should be a crossing guard at such a big and busy intersection, but then something happened that she was sure her husband would never believe. All the children stopped talking to each other and stood waiting at the curb. She saw the huge dog with the cat on his head seem to look from side to side, up and down the street as if he was checking for traffic. Then he walked into the middle of the street and sat down. He nodded toward the children, and they began to move into the street. Gwen took her mother's hand.

"It's OK, Mom. It's safe to cross now." They had only taken a step or two into the street when a car came fast around the corner. The other children seemed to pay no attention to the approaching car, but Mrs. Nelson could not help herself. She had to try to pull her daughter out of the way of danger. She heard the car's brakes squeal and smelled rubber as it came to a lurching stop. Only then did she realize that the dog had been watching the children, but that the cat had turned toward the car. There seemed to be some kind of bright green light in the cat's eyes.

"Come on, Mom. It's safe." Her daughter pulled at her arm again. Mrs. Nelson could not help but look angrily at the young woman behind the wheel of the car whose tires were smoking and smelled of burned rubber. The young woman rubbed and shook her head as if she suddenly had some kind of horrible headache, but still she called out from her open window, "You are so right, Anthony and Miss C. I wasn't paying attention, and I was going way too fast. All the kids are OK, aren't they? You stopped me in time, didn't you, Miss C? I am so sorry. I promise it won't happen again."

What could a mother do except take a deep breath, hold her daughter's hand, and walk into the street? When she reached Anthony and Cleopatra, who were still sitting in the street, she stopped for a moment to take a closer and better look at them. The dog, though large, seemed like a regular dog. She had seen pictures of dogs like him, and she was pretty sure that they were called Mastiffs. When she looked at The Cat, she could only think that even without the earrings and other jewelry—she had never seen a cat like her before. But as she passed by them, she felt a soft paw reach out and touch her hand. She turned in surprise and saw the greenest eyes she had ever seen looking back at her. She then felt a sensation of trust come over her as she heard the words, "Your child will always be safe with us."

The other children quickly broke the spell, telling them to hurry because they could see the school bus coming at the far end of the street. The dog and cat did not move until everyone was safe on the other side of the street. Only then did the driver of the car, still rubbing her head, begin to drive very slowly up the street. Mrs. Nelson left her daughter with hugs, kisses, wishes for a great day, and a prayer for her to meet new friends. The bus pulled away, but when she looked up through the window, she saw Gwen laughing and smiling.

As she headed back home, the dog and cat walked beside her until she arrived at her house. She stopped and stroked Anthony's ear. "Thank you so much, very big dog." Then she looked up at Cleopatra and added, "And very strange cat." Mrs. Nelson walked up her driveway, thinking that she was never going to be able to explain this to her husband. Maybe she should not even try.

⌒〠〝

That afternoon when Gwen got off the school bus, she was very happy to see Anthony and Cleopatra sitting there, waiting for her and all the other children, but she was surprised that her mother was not there. "Oh, well," she thought. Her mother was probably stuck in traffic someplace and would be there in a minute or two. There was nothing for her to worry about. This had been a great day at her new school. It might have been her very best first day at a new school ever. Jeffrey had even found her and sat with her for lunch, and boys never did anything like that.

As she walked down the street, following behind the dog and cat, she thought about all her friends at her last school and how much she missed them, especially her one very special friend, Athena, but maybe this new place might not be that bad after all. Gwen felt her cell phone vibrate in her pocket. It was her mom.

"Honey, you can probably tell I'm not at home waiting for you. I'm stuck in traffic on this highway they call The Beltway. You know, the one that goes all around Washington. I feel like a hamster going around in a wheel. I'll be there as soon as I can."

"Don't worry, Mom. It's a nice day, and I'll be fine." You learned two rules of life when you were an MK, a Military Kid. Rule Number One: Stuff Happens. Rule Number Two: You learn to deal with stuff. Gwen had waited for her parents before but never for very long, and it was a nice day, not raining or cold. She could sit on the steps and begin doing her homework. She didn't know why, but she turned to Anthony and Cleopatra, who had just left Jeffrey and Bobby at their house and continued to walk with her until they reached her house. "Thanks for walking me home, guys. My mom's going to be late getting back, so I'm going to sit here and do some homework while I wait for her."

The little girl's heart almost stopped when she heard, "That is all right. Our Boys are at home with The Mother, so we will stay here with you until your mother arrives."

Gwen could only stand almost frozen in place and stare at *The Big Dog*. "Did you just talk to me? Did I just hear you talk?"

"Well, of course, you did, Gwen. We can talk to all children, and all children can talk to us," said the reassuring voice of Anthony.

"Of course, if they are horrible children, The Noble Anthony might talk to them, but I will not. I only reward good children with knowledge of me. You seem to be very good and very nice," Cleopatra added. "So I will talk with you."

Gwen thought that she knew a lot of things for a nine-year-old, but this was something very different. She found herself sitting down hard onto her front steps.

Then Cleopatra went on, "The Noble Anthony and I will stay with you until your mother arrives. You should call your mother and let her know that we are with you. After this morning, she will know that means you are safe. If she is later than she expects to be, Jeffrey and Bobby's mother will come and join us. She will talk to your mother, and then you will go home with us until your mother arrives."

Gwen closed her homework book and looked at the two of them. "Well, if we're going to spend this time together, I would like to know some things about the two of you—like how did you get this ability to talk to kids? Is it just kids, or can you talk to grown-ups too? Where did you come from, and how long have you been together?"

Cleopatra looked deep into the girl's eyes and then at Anthony. They did not say anything to each other, and Gwen could not hear their thoughts. They just nodded to each other and then turned back to Gwen.

"We will tell you, but you will only be able to share our story with one other person. That person will not be your father or mother. It will only be when you become an adult and you find the person with whom you will share your life. That is the only one you will be able to tell about the special ability you have with us. Do you accept this?"

Gwen planned to say something like "Sure" or "That's fine," but instead she heard herself say, "Of course, My Lady. It shall be as you command." The little girl was about to protest that it was not her answer, but then she thought that maybe she should just be quiet and listen to the story.

The Noble Anthony began. "My Lady and I have been together since the time of the Pharaohs in ancient Egypt. We lived together in The Temple of The Goddess Bastet, who has the body of a human woman but the beautiful face of a cat. It was a time of great wisdom and knowledge among humans, for they knew cats to be a sacred gift to humans from all the other gods. I was one of the guardians of The Temple and all who lived and worked there."

Cleopatra continued, "There came a time when The Noble Anthony and I left The Temple. We were asked to live in the home of one of the human Priestesses. She had a husband and two small children, a boy and a girl, and we stayed with this family for several years. We grew to love them as they grew to love us. We watched over them, and one night the parents went out and left their children in our care. It was during this time, thinking for some reason that The Priestess would have treasures from The Temple in her own home, two thieves broke into the house. At first the men were willing to take whatever they could find that might be of some small value and leave. When they realized the boy and girl would be able to say who they were, they sought to do terrible harm to them."

Cleopatra's voice had begun to tremble, and her deep green eyes had blurred with tears, as if what she was going to say next was still too horrible, even centuries later, for her to bear. She looked up from Gwen into the face of The Mastiff beside her and continued, "Of course, The Great Love of My Life, The Noble Anthony, could not allow that to happen, and so to protect the children, he attacked the two men. I called unto The Goddess Bastet to please help keep My Beloved from harm." Again Cleopatra stopped, and this time she used her paw to wipe away her tears. She was almost unable to speak when she began again.

"One of the men had a knife, and before The Goddess could respond, he inflicted a mortal wound onto My Beloved Anthony. The men ran off into the night, but the children were safe. I threw myself onto My Beloved, and I heard his great heartbeat for the final time. The pain of losing My Anthony was so great to me that my own heart broke in two, and I also died that night as I lay on him."

"You died?" the girl heard herself say. "The two of you died?" Gwen realized that tears were running down her face. Without thinking about what she was doing, she reached out and picked The Cat up, held her to her chest, and began to pet her. Both The Child and The Cat once again felt the loss of the ones whom they had loved—Gwen, mourning the loss of her friend Athena, and Cleopatra, reliving the loss of Her Beloved. Anthony moved closer to them and kissed both The Girl and His Beloved with his huge tongue to comfort them. They quieted, both receiving comfort from each other and *The Big Dog*.

Still sitting on Gwen's lap, Cleopatra continued, "Anthony and I did truly die that day as all things must and do, but then we awoke. We were together, but it was a different time, and we were in a different place. The Goddess Bastet, to reward us for our sacrifice, had returned us to life."

Anthony continued for her, "That is how it began and how it has continued until this time. We awaken, and we come to a new place and to a new family that has children. We stay with each family for all the years while the children grow up. When they are ready to go off and make their own way in the world and maybe have families of their own, we die, as all pets of families do. The parents and the now grown-up children mourn us. They remember us and tell stories of happy times with us. Then we go on to be with a new family and new children."

At first Gwen could only say, "Wow," but then it came to her. "So the talking. How are we able to talk to each other? I've had friends who had pets, and the people talked to their pets, but no dog, cat, hamster, or ferret ever talked back, and the people sure didn't understand the sounds the animals made."

"That too," The Noble Anthony explained, "was part of the gift from The Goddess. Children usually can communicate with us after a few hours. It was a bit unusual that the ability surprised you."

"But maybe that is because you are special," Cleopatra said. "This friend that you had to leave, this Athena. Was she very special to you?"

"Oh yes," answered Gwen, almost starting to cry again. "Athena and I would laugh and play at each others houses. We would sing songs together and dance. I could tell her things that I've never even told my mom, and she wouldn't say mean things to me or think that some of the things that I like are silly. Some of the other girls seem to want to grow up so fast and wear lipstick and act crazy over boys and talk about going to dances and things like that. Athena and I, we enjoyed being little girls. We love fairies and going horseback riding and waiting up for Santa Claus. I like those things, and

Athena did too. Our parents are planning to let us talk and see each other on the computer once a week. We will be able to talk about school and stuff, but it's not the same as being with her."

Cleopatra reached up with her paw and wiped the tears from The Child's face. "You know what, My Anthony? You have Your Boys whom you go off and play with. I think the time has come for me to have a friend too. I will be your friend, Gwen. Do you like tea parties?"

Gwen hugged the cat and squealed with delight. "I love tea parties. Athena and I would have them all the time. We wore wonderful hats and everything."

"Well, my tea parties might be a little different, and there are a few rules. Unless I tell you not to, you may pet me at any time, except for my tummy. You can only rub my tummy when I give you permission. Now, at the tea parties, there can be no chocolate because that can be dangerous for both dogs and cats. There can also be no milk or cream. I do not know why humans started giving cow milk to cats. Cow milk is for growing baby cows into big cows. It is not for growing cats into anything. Milk does very unpleasant things to our tummies, so no milk. Now, sometimes The Noble Anthony might want to join us, so you will need to have a special treat for him."

In her excitement, Gwen broke in. "Oh, will he wear a big floppy hat with lots of flowers on it?"

Cleopatra had visions of Sniffer and his ever-changing ear ribbons. She said firmly, "Only if he should desire to, but you have to remove it before we go home." The thought of The Boys falling over with laughter at the sight of The Noble Anthony in a floppy flowered hat did not rest well with her. "Now I would like to be served sautéed worm…"

She could feel Anthony's steely look. She gave him a narrow-eyed look back but then continued most graciously, "I would like to be served anything that you and your mother choose. I will bring my own hat. We can talk and laugh, and you can tell me anything. After all, the entire universe knows that what is discussed at a tea party, is never, mentioned elsewhere."

"Will you go on the computer with me so that Athena can see you too?"

"If you wish, I will do this thing for you."

"Will you talk to Athena too?" This time Gwen sounded less sure of herself when she asked.

"That will be up to you. You can share this part of me with her, or you may keep it unto yourself." Then The Cat rubbed the side of her face against that of The Girl, marking Gwen as her own. She pressed her head against the little girl's chest and began to purr.

"And I promise you this, My Gwen: you and Athena will make other friends and have good times with them. As you get older, time and circumstances may cause you to drift apart. Do not be sad about it, because you will always have the memory of the very special friendship that the two of you shared. These will be the stories you will share with others as you grow, and later you will share these stories of love and friendship with your own children. So know this, My Dear One: whether Athena is near or far away, she will always be a very important part of who you are." Cleopatra turned and looked up the street to quickly break the spell. "Now, I think that is your mother coming."

Even though Gwen had called her mother and told her that Anthony and Cleopatra were waiting with her, Mrs. Nelson was still surprised to see the three of them sitting on the front steps. Surprised and happy that her daughter had not had to wait alone. There were hugs and kisses all around, and Gwen excitedly told her mother that she and Cleopatra would be having tea parties together and that maybe they could do them on the computer so Athena could join in too. When she had put her daughter on the school bus that morning, her silent prayer had been that Gwen would find a friend. Of course, she had not expected the friend to be the strange jewelry-wearing cat. Gwen seemed happier than she had been in a while, so her mother could only be pleased. Mrs. Nelson sighed and asked Gwen what she would like for dinner. She decided that a strange cat friend was better than no friend at all.

As Gwen went into the house with her mother, Anthony, with Cleopatra on his head as usual, began the walk down the street to their house. They had not gone far when The Big Dog stopped and stared at a white van that was parked in the next block.

"It is those men again. The ones whom I smelled a few days ago on our way to The Great Alexander's Pronouncement. They are the ones who do not smell right."

He continued walking past their house and up the street until they were right across from the van. Two men were sitting in it, and when the one in the driver's seat saw them, he nudged his companion and pointed at the dog and cat.

"They have never seen us before," Cleopatra whispered. Everyone in Bowie knew about Anthony and Cleopatra—from going to the farmers' market or to church in the summer when it was held outside, and of course story reading time at the local library, definitely from attending Bowiefest, or just from walking the children to the bus. The Cat and The Dog were known and accepted. No one pointed at them, and no one laughed at them. "I am not sure that I like these men. Maybe I should turn them into—"

"My Lovely, we have just been through that. They do not know us, and we do not know them. That does not mean that they are bad or have done anything wrong. There is something frighteningly familiar about them, though, and I don't like them being so close to the house and to My Boys." Anthony breathed their scent in deeply once again. "I will remember them. I may even ask Sniffer if he has noticed them, because his nose is stronger than mine, but for right now, My Lady, we must go home. The Mother will be wondering where we are, and I need to know what My Boys are up to."

"Yes, and I will let The Mother know we will soon be having tea parties. Who knows, maybe The Lady Emma-Gene will need to make you a new hat, My Love. Something floppy with a few flowers on it."

Welcome to Bowiefest

Fitzwallace was pacing back and forth impatiently on his perch. Where in the world was his human, David? What was taking him so long to get here? Didn't David know there was so much to do this day? First, he would need his shower. His feathers had to be super clean so they would glisten in the sun today, and, of course, his talons had to be cleaned, filed, and polished. Fitzwallace would be wearing his new hood today. It was leather, and it had black, red, white, and yellow streamers flowing from the top like a river of color. He would be wearing all the colors of the Maryland state flag. He had to look his very best today; after all he was a falcon, and he was going to be the star of the show.

Two years ago, Fitzwallace had thought for sure that he was going to die. He had been wounded by a group of boys carelessly playing with a BB gun. They were shooting up into the air, thinking that it was fun and harmless, and they did not even see him come crashing to the ground. He was frightened and in horrible pain. Falcons do not spend a lot of time on the ground. Wounded and unable to fly, he knew that he could quickly become dinner for some other animal. He somehow managed to make it through the night, but by morning, he was cold, tired, and very weak. He heard footsteps coming toward him through the woods, and he was sure his life would soon be over. He had been wrong.

The footsteps were those of David and Ellen Miller. They had been taking a walk along one of the many bike trails on a lovely autumn day. They probably would not have even noticed the wounded bird if they had not heard the rustling of the leaves as he made a last desperate attempt to get away. Ellen put her scarf over his eyes to calm him, and she and David took him to a special bird veterinarian. After an examination and x-rays, the doctor told David and Ellen that although he could set the wing and it would heal, it would never be strong enough for the falcon to fly again. Since that would mean that he could not be released back into the wild and experience the life of a wild falcon again, the doctor had suggested that maybe it might be better to put the bird to sleep.

Fortunately, for Fitzwallace, he had been found by two very special people. David and Ellen had been trained and licensed by The State of Maryland to own and operate a wildlife show. They lovingly kept several animals that they took to schools and other events to help teach children to love, respect, and appreciate all the wild things that lived in the woods. At their home, they had an opossum, a raccoon, bunnies, and several snakes that you might find in your garden. They thought the falcon would be a great addition to their "animal family." They adopted the wounded falcon and named him Fitzwallace. With love and tender care, Fitzwallace became well and strong in a few months. David built a huge enclosure for him. No, living in an enclosure was not the same as soaring through the sky on a beautiful autumn day, but the falcon was alive. He received good food every day, and there were walkways, a perch, and landings that his weak wing could still fly him to. David was kind and had taught the bird how to wear a hood so that he would not see things and become frightened. Fitzwallace had also learned how to stand and look majestic and handsome on David's gloved arm. Today he and David were going to be the very first thing that people would see as they opened and welcomed everyone to *Bowiefest*!

Since 1977, the City of Bowie had celebrated itself as a perfect place to live, work, and raise a family. On the first Saturday in June, the residents of Bowie and the surrounding communities would gather at Allen Pond for a day of fun and relaxation. There were tables and grills for picnicking. Activities like baton twirling, sand art, a pie-eating contest for dogs, and even a dog fashion show. Rides for the children and paddleboats to take out on the pond. Food vendors of every possible type and information booths showing off the services of the city and the wares and services of businesses and local houses of worship. All attending were encouraged to bring their pets, and David and Ellen would be there with Fitzwallace and their other animals.

⌒⋔⋔⌒

Michael and Michelle Wilkinson loved Bowiefest and had been going there ever since they were kids themselves. They had been taking Jeffrey and Bobby since they were babies, and once Anthony had become part of The

Family, there had been no stopping The Father from showing off his *BIG DOG*. There was no Biggest-Dog Contest, but Michael Wilkinson was certain that, even though Sebastian the Great Dane might be the tallest dog, his English Mastiff would be The Biggest, and The Noble Anthony would still win first prize. That morning, everyone was busy getting ready for the big day. The Father was polishing the silver band on Anthony's collar for the fifth time. The Mother was putting the finishing touches on a basket of goodies to share with some friends and neighbors and, at the same time, wondering what Cleopatra would want to wear. Jeffrey and Bobby were just being boys and having a good time with Anthony.

Finally The Mother called out, "Come on, My Lady. We have to get you dressed so that we can leave soon."

The Mother went into the laundry/dressing room, only to find the cat sitting on the counter waiting for her. "I should have known you would already be here, My Lady. You're as excited to go as we are, but I think that your reason is to see your friends again. Anyway, let's get you ready."

Even though Michelle had seen her cat's wardrobe a thousand times, it still surprised her to see the extent of it. Maybe Michael had been right when he said that Cleopatra had more clothes than most humans. In fact, just a few days ago, she had found a gigantic, humongous life jacket and a little tiny one on the laundry room counter, thanks, of course, to Auntie Emma-Gene. The big one was for Anthony and the smaller one for Cleopatra. Auntie had felt that they should have them for the summer Sundays when The Family rented a sailboat in Annapolis and went out together onto the Chesapeake Bay. After all, the humans wore life jackets, so why shouldn't they, or so said Auntie.

"All right, My Lady. We have to get going; so what will your pleasure be today?" The Mother said, as she gestured to the many items. "You know, a lot of people at Bowiefest today will be looking forward to seeing you, so how about giving them a show with the gold cape and crown?"

Cleopatra looked at The Mother lovingly but gently shook her head no.

"You're right; too showy. How about the red cape and gold collar?"

Another head shake.

"You're right again, My Lady. Still too showy, and it's going to be hot out there today."

The Cat's paw pointed to the red and white bandanna hanging on its peg.

"Are you sure you want this one? I think you wore this one last year."

Again The Cat touched the peg with the red and white bandanna.

"OK, whatever you say. You're the boss, or in this case, The Lady. So do you want the straw hat too?"

The cat nodded.

"And what about sunglasses? The sun is going to be brutal today. We'll be using lots of sunscreen. Oh, and, of course, the gold hoop earrings?"

With everything approved, the cat was dressed in just a moment. "Of course, now that you're ready, where is Anthony?"

"Mom, Mom," The Boys were calling as they came near. "Mom, look what we did. We got Anthony all dressed too."

There he was. The not quite so noble-looking Anthony was wearing big sunglasses and a huge straw hat on his big head. The Boys had cut a hole on one side of the hat to let his ear hang out but had forgotten to do so on the other side, so THE BIG DOG had a rather lopsided look to him. The Boys looked at The Mother with such pride in their accomplishment that she did not have the courage or heart to mention the other ear. She did, however, have to mention one other rather important thing.

"Where is Cleopatra going to sit? You know that she's not going to walk on the grass or on the dirt any more than she has to."

"Oh, we thought of that. All we have to do is this." Bobby took both his hands and crushed the top of the hat flat down onto Anthony's head. "Now she'll sit right there."

There was no getting around it. It was not pretty, but it would work. The Mother could only shake her head and congratulate the two beaming faces grinning up at her. "Good work, guys, and a job well done. Let's go get Dad and hit the road."

They all walked into the kitchen, where they found The Father, who had just finished polishing Anthony's collar. He was admiring his work once again when he saw Cleopatra come in wearing her straw hat, sunglasses, and red and white bandanna. He stopped what he was doing and said, "She's not going to wear that, is she?"

"Of course, she is," answered The Mother, coming to The Lady's defense. "It's going to be very hot out there today, and she looks wonderful." Michelle had also tried to add an air of warning to her voice.

"Well, you would think that with all those clothes in there she could come up with something better for Bowiefest. After all, there are going to be a lot of people there, so if she's going to wear clothes, she might as well look good. There will be people there who know me."

The Mother just looked at her husband and shook her head. "Boys, come on and let's get going. Anthony, do you have the basket of Frisbees? We better all get into the van before something horrible happens to your father."

⌒⋀⌒

One of the good things about Bowiefest was that Allen Pond was only about fifteen minutes away from home. One of the bad things was that everyone had the same idea of arriving early in order to get a good parking place. So even thirty minutes before the official opening, the parking lot was already a sea of cars.

"See, I told you that we were never going to find a parking space," The Father grumbled. "The only way we'll get a spot today that is still within the city limits will be if someone dies and leaves us one in their will."

"Well, Dad," pitched in Jeffrey, "this lady must be leaving for the funeral, because she just pulled out two cars behind us."

As The Father turned around to look out of the back window so that he could reverse into the space, he caught a glimpse of Cleopatra, and he was almost certain that she was sticking her tongue out at him.

"All right. We're going to head over to that stand of trees over there. The Men's Club from church will be cooking barbecue, and I'll be helping them. You guys can help your mother set up the table and get ready for lunch. I don't know what the rest of you are going to do after that, but your mother and I," he said, giving his wife a quick smile, "have a date at the paddleboats."

"Sure, Dad, we know." Bobby was getting Anthony's basket of Frisbees out of the back. "Are you feeling OK now?"

"Of course, I do. I'm just fine." This probably would have gone over better if he had not been rubbing his shoulder when he said it. It was the same shoulder that would have a beauty of a black and blue mark on it by that time the next day.

"Well, dear, you did take quite a fall," The Mother said, as she straightened Cleopatra's straw hat. "Thank goodness, it was on the lawn, or we would be at The Health Center right now. I can't imagine where the cat toy that you tripped over came from. We don't even have any cat toys like that. But I'm sure," The Mother said, giving her husband another warning look, "that you will now agree that Cleopatra looks wonderful just the way that she is. Doesn't she?"

"Yes, yes, she looks fine," he grumbled. "So are we going to stand here all day? We're at Bowiefest, for Pete's sake. Let's get going."

Anthony was already out of the van but was backing himself up against the front seat. When he had himself perfectly level with it, Cleopatra got up and carefully stepped onto his back. Then she walked the length of his body and settled herself right into the perfect nest that Bobby had made for her in Anthony's straw hat. Once settled in, she nodded to everyone to indicate that she was ready to go.

There were people of every size, shape, color, and age for as far as the eye could see. Ducks and geese in the pond were swimming up to the paddleboat riders looking for goodies. Grandparents were sitting on blankets under the trees, sharing pictures with their friends. Parents were pushing babies in strollers and trying to keep up with toddlers. Groups of people moved from booth to booth buying food, crafts, and artwork. And, of course, along the way people stopped to look at the cat who was riding around on top of a dog's head. Some people who knew them waved and called out greetings while pointing them out to their visiting friends and relatives. Cleopatra made sure that Anthony stopped for a bit every now and then so that everyone could see and admire her. Being adored by the crowd was almost like being back at The Temple of Bastet, except now the people could also take pictures.

Finally she said, "Let us move on, My Beloved. That will have to be enough for right now. They can take more pictures before we leave. Right now I am excited and want to see our friends."

They had only gone a little farther when Anthony said, "Look, My Lovely, there is Ares with Drake and Miss Martha lying over there by the edge of the pond." He was directing her gaze toward a yellow shepherd and Lab mix lying beside his constant companions, the handsome Mallard, Drake and his lovely full-figured white domestic duck wife, Miss Martha. "Strange, though. Ares is usually known as The Green-Legged Dog, but for some reason today he seems to be green all the way up to his neck. I will have to remember to ask him about that later." The ducks waved their wings in greeting as Anthony and His Lady walked by.

Of course, when Cleopatra had spoken of seeing their friends, The Lusty Tara Tupa had not been whom she had in mind. The black Lab had seemed to appear out of nowhere, smiling and wagging her tail so hard that she was actually wagging her entire body. Tara Tupa still had her eyes on Anthony, and the excitement of the day had made her bold. "Anthony!" she called out to him, and she waggled herself toward them.

Anthony turned his head slowly in her direction, with Cleopatra sitting in the middle of his crushed straw hat. "Tara Tupa, how nice to see you again. Is your family with you?"

"Oh yes, they're at that table over there." She could hardly point her nose in that direction because her hind end was wagging so fast. "I'd heard that you walk around town with that Fur Ball sitting on your head, but I didn't want to believe it. And this time it's even wearing sunglasses."

Even through the crushed hat on his head, Anthony could still feel Cleopatra's claws just barely grazing his skin.

"Tara Tupa," she said, the sunglasses hiding the icy look of her green eyes, "how nice to see that you have recovered so well from that unfortunate case of mange you had."

The horrible skin infection dogs sometimes get had caused most of the black Lab's fur to fall out, and the itching had been just awful. Her human mother had even had to tie socks onto her feet to keep the dog from scratching herself too badly, which had only made her look even more ridiculous with the huge plastic "Cone of Shame" she was already wearing around her neck. To make matters even worse, the treatment for the condition had been daily baths in the most foul-smelling concoction ever known to human or beast.

As she remembered the treatments, fear and embarrassment quickly replaced the smile on Tara Tupa's face, and she tucked the frantically wagging tail tightly beneath her. "My Mommy said that wasn't my fault. My Mommy said I'm a good girl, and I didn't do anything to deserve that. I'm a good girl," she whimpered in reply.

"Of course, you are, my dear. In fact, I think I hear your human Mommy calling you now. It must be bath time again. Run along now, my dear. We would not want to have all your fur fall out again, now would we?"

The Lab turned, quickly ran back to her human parents, and once again tried to climb into someone's arms.

"My Lovely, please tell me that you did not—" Anthony asked.

"Of course not, My Darling. It was just a very happy coincidence, though I do feel certain that baths every day would have been a wonderful experience for her. Now let us move on and see who else is here."

Just as the food vendors and the people selling crafts had their own locations around the pond, there was also a holding area for some of the pets when they were not walking with their humans. First, they visited The Greyhounds. Cleopatra loved The Greyhounds. They were direct descendants of the dogs of ancient Egypt. Even though they were the second-fastest animals on the earth, they were gentle and loving creatures. The tall, sleek dogs enjoyed being with each other, and they were known for their quiet and stately manner. So it was quite a surprise to the group when a new fawn-colored hound barked excitedly at the sight of Cleopatra and immediately incurred the scorn of all the others.

Instantly feeling their displeasure, the new dog lowered his head, averted its eyes, and sputtered, "Oh my goodness. Was that me? Oh, I'm so sorry. It seems to have just slipped out. Please, I beg your pardon. Please forgive me."

Dowland, the senior Greyhound of the group, walked over to Anthony and Cleopatra, slightly bowed his head, and said, "Please do forgive him, My

Lady. He is young and new to the group. I assure you that he meant no disrespect and that it will not happen again."

"It is fine, Dowland. No harm was done, and no offense was taken. We were all young and new at one time, were we not? It is good to see you and all the others, including the new one," Cleopatra said sweetly, as she gently and lovingly stroked her paw against the long pointy noses that were presented to her by the other Greyhounds.

"You are gracious and forgiving as always, My Lady." The older dog stepped back out of the way and let Anthony pass.

They had only taken a few steps when Scout and his daughter, Reagan, trotted up to them. The two black Newfoundlands, who were natural water and rescue dogs, had just arrived with their family. The dogs were anxious to start patrolling the perimeters of the pond for any trouble. The two big long-haired dogs were already wearing their lifesaving vests, which had loops and handles on them so distressed swimmers could grab hold of them. They were also trained to dive and come up underneath an unconscious person. Their loving and supportive human parents were with them, carrying their life preservers just in case they might be needed.

"Anthony, My Lady, good to see you before we start our patrol," said the big shaggy Scout. "My little girl and I will be on the lookout all day, you know. True, there is no swimming allowed on the pond, but you never know what can happen with those paddleboats. We've got to be ever alert and ever ready, I always say. Must be on our way now. Good to see you again. Here's to a peaceful and uneventful Bowiefest." And with a quick flip of their tails, they were gone.

Even before they got close to it, Anthony and Cleopatra could already tell who was at the big table ahead of them because of all the humans standing around. It could only be The Infamous Buda Kalie. The white, orange, and gray calico cat was famous throughout all of Bowie and certain parts of the county for being the most notorious Cat Burglar in the past fifty years. No one, not even her humans, knew exactly how old she was, but she was thought to be somewhere between twenty or thirty years old, and she weighed at least twenty-seven pounds. Though she was supposedly retired now, in her day, nothing and no one was safe from her roaming, day or night.

Some people had gone as far as saying that she had keys to almost every house in Bowie.

As the story goes, she began innocently enough with her family. She would take towels, pencils, socks, car keys, her human Mom's wedding ring, a bag of the dog's treats, or the wayward kid's toy. To the family, it seemed cute, innocent, and even amusing. She put all of her treasures in her special nest under her human parents' bed. When her human mother caught on to this and began retrieving the missing items, the huge, lumbering cat started to move on to the neighbors. At that point she really came into her own. She brought home dolls, teddy bears, bathing suits, shoes, garden tools, newspapers, and a wallet or two. Her humans began to have a monthly Lost and Found Day so that people could come by and claim their lost items. It was rumored that one summer she brought home a bicycle, a hammock, a complete outdoor set of chairs and the matching table, and a riding lawn mower. And, of course, no one would ever forget the Sunday morning when her humans woke to find a small child sitting at the foot of their bed beside the laughing cat.

Today she was lying on her back on her chaise lounge, showing off her magnificent belly to the world. Beside her was the usual "touch the belly at your own risk" sign, just in case there was someone new in town. The sign had been added a few years ago after an unfortunate incident with a visiting grandmother who had never mastered the concept of looking but not touching. Of course, the grandmother now knew better.

The old cat had on her usual pearl necklace, her big floppy straw hat with the flowers all over it, and to protect her large yellow eyes from the sun, cat-eye sunglasses. Beside her was a glass with a long bent straw that reached over to her so she could sip iced tea, flavored with catnip, of course.

"My Lady," the old cat called out, "I really like those earrings you're wearing."

"Thank you, Buda Kalie," Cleopatra replied. "I like them too, and I would like to keep them."

"Oh, that's a good one, My Lady." The old cat cackled as The Dog and The Cat walked by, and she slapped her paws against her huge belly to show her enjoyment. "Yes, that's a really good one."

Anthony didn't say anything, but he was certain he heard the clinking of the cat going through her hidden pile of keys.

〰〰

As Anthony and Cleopatra continued, they passed Sebastian, the harlequin Great Dane, and his lovely wife, Julia, a black-and-white Boston Grate Dane. Since the Danes belonged to The Father's best friend, Hakeem Price, and the two couples saw each other often, they could pass each other today with just a nod and a smile and save their time for others whom they only saw at the festival.

Not far away was something very new this year. A large clear glass tank full of water encased Andy The Anaconda for all to see and admire. Even though the twenty-five-foot-long snake supposedly lovingly embraced his human family, the festival committee decided that this year, he should be confined to the water tank after the unfortunate disappearance of Guinea and Pig the previous year. After all, he had been questioned once by the police when a small child went missing for a few hours.

Anthony stopped so that Cleopatra could talk to the anaconda for a moment. "Now, Andy, you must tell me, what did happen to Guinea and Pig last year?"

"S-s-s-s-s-s-s-s, not to worry, My Lovely Lady. They are s-s-still here with me." He turned and touched his head to the still rather large lump in one of his giant coils. "In fact, Noble Anthony, look into my eyes and bring The Lady closer s-s-so that s-s-s-s-he might s-s-s-s-ee for hers-s-s-self."

Anthony immediately took several steps away from the snake. Everyone, except possibly Guinea and Pig, knew not to get too close to Andy and to never ever look directly into his eyes.

"Oh, you are no fun at all." The big snake laughed in his strange hissing way.

"Anthony, My Beloved, I think that we should move on now," Cleopatra said to her husband, trying to sound confident and in command.

"You are right as usual, My Lady." And The Big Mastiff continued along the path.

In the background they could see Rocky J. Wood, the white-and-gray-striped tabby who was known to her friends as The Rock. She had begun as an ordinary rescued house pet. She had even had a litter of babies, and it was said that she was a wonderful and caring mother. Then, at the ripe old age of nine, she began to hunt and became The Provider for Her Family. She had started out small with mice and moles. Her human family even teased her for being the great huntress of blind things. This only caused the nine-pound cat to up her game, and she began to bring home chipmunks that were alive and got loose in the house, bunnies that had to be rescued and released, and finally her crowning glory, a ten-point buck, which the family found on their front porch one afternoon and which really freaked out the UPS lady.

Hunting is not for everyone, even cats, whom some people think are born hunters. The Rock was now thirteen years old, and the signs of her escapades were visible. She wore an eye patch, was missing a right front leg, and walked with a crutch because of her back peg leg, and her tail was bent in about four different places. Obviously not all of her prey came along willingly. Still, she let her friends know she had not given up and was still on the lookout to bring home a buffalo one day. It was rumored that the UPS lady had heard of this and decided to take a job at an ice-cream shop. The Rock's human family members were relieved to know that so far there never had been a buffalo in Bowie.

The Noble Anthony and His Lady finished the circular path around the pond just in time to see Sniffer holding his head high as he carried the basket carrying his kitten, The Great Alexander. Of course, Sniffer's Twin Girls had decorated the basket with red, black, yellow, and white ribbons, signifying the Maryland state flag. Sniffer had ribbons of the same colors on his ears and tail, but this time he did not seem to mind at all. In fact, many felt that the tiara balanced carefully on his head and the tutu safety-pinned around his middle really set off his look.

"Sniffer," The Big Mastiff called out to him. "I will speak to you about this later, but I have noticed the scent of two new men in the neighborhood. They are usually in a white van. I do not know why, but there is something about their scent that is familiar to me, and it gives me an uneasy feeling."

The Bloodhound stopped beside Anthony and gently put his kitten's basket down on the ground. "Good day, Miss Cleo. You're lookin' mighty fine this morning."

"And so are you, Sniffer. In fact you look quite exceptional today."

Feeling that he had been given a great compliment, he smiled and said, "Well, thank you, ma'am. My Girls do go all out for Bowiefest, you know." He turned his attention to Anthony. "I know the two that you mean. I've noticed their scent too. It's not one that I remember from anything else, but there is something about it that I don't like. I've talked to Rosie and her sister Poise. You know, one of them is black and white, and the other is brown and white. I can never remember which is which. But their humans like to exercise and do a lot of walking and running all over town, and they've found the scent of those men all over the place."

"That's interesting to know." Anthony tried not to show too much concern.

"One last thing." Sniffer stepped closer to The Big Dog, as if he were trying to keep Cleopatra, who, of course, was sitting right on Anthony's head, from hearing "They also said that they had heard their humans talking about two homes that had been broken into not far away. I don't have any way of knowing if it was these two men, but I thought that you might want to know."

Anthony could not help taking in a deep breath to check their present location. Yes, everything was fine there, for the moment anyway. "Thank you, Sniffer. That is indeed something that I should know." He brushed his head against that of the other dog, each marking the other as a friend. "We will all have to be on the lookout, but for today, I think that we can have some fun." Sniffer nodded and then picked up his kitten's basket and continued down the path.

"Anthony? Is there something to be concerned about?"

He could hear the uneasiness in his Beloved's voice. "At this time, My Lady, there is nothing to worry about. I only wish that I could remember where I had come across their scent before, but here we are with The Family. So for now we will enjoy the day."

Finally they returned to The Family's table for some much-needed lunch and water. The Boys were looking forward to an after-lunch game of Keep-Away-Catch-Return, with the other dogs and some of the dads using the basket of Frisbees that Anthony had brought. The game had been given this name because some of the dogs would really catch and return the plastic disk, while others would keep it and run away with it. Many large-breed dogs do not play with Frisbees because they are not as fast as the smaller breeds and because the jumping and landing can be very hard on their joints, but Anthony loved to play. It was a true and beautiful sight to behold the Mighty Mastiff jumping high into the air, turning, and twisting as he grabbed the plastic disk in his mouth. He almost seemed to swallow it. The smaller and so-called faster breeds found themselves hard-pressed to keep up.

After listening to Mayor Robinson do his annual Welcome to Bowiefest speech, The Father and Mother planned to take a nice quiet ride together on the paddleboats, knowing that The Boys would be safe with Anthony and the other dads. Even though it meant she would have to walk by herself on the ground, through the grass, and maybe even on the dirt paths, Cleopatra knew of a hidden spot where she could lay unseen and enjoy the quiet while she watched all the activities away from everyone. The hidden spot was near a large oak tree not far from the pier that jutted out into the pond. Normally she was not fond of lying on the ground, but the grass under the low hanging greenery was soft, and the sun had warmed the ground. She could be unseen and yet still watch the paddleboats go by. It was not the same as gliding down the Nile River of Egypt in her own barge, listening to the sound of the oars dipping in and out of the water and the pounding of the drum that helped the rowers keep the rhythm, but it was still nice.

Most families did not set up their table or blanket in that area, so she was somewhat surprised to see both under the oak tree. Even more surprising was a father asleep under the tree with his young baby in his arms. At least she thought that he was the father, since he was surrounded by a baby stroller, a baby bag, a package of diapers, and several baby toys. Knowing some of the ways of humans, Cleopatra guessed the child had been left in the care of its father while the mother took a few minutes to go and enjoy some of the craft tables and maybe bring back some homemade ice cream to share. Since both were asleep and reasonably quiet, even though she thought the father might have been snoring just a little bit, The Cat did not think they would disturb her enjoyment at all, so she settled into her hidden spot. Away from the noise of the people and relaxed by the warmth of the sun, Cleopatra had drifted off to sleep for a few minutes herself.

Her slumber was interrupted by the playful gurgling sounds coming from under the oak tree. The baby was awake. The baby was awake, and the baby's father was still asleep. The baby was no longer lying in its father's arms. It was sitting a few feet away from the still-snoring man, and it was happily talking to itself and playfully pulling at the grass. The child seemed content and pretty quiet for a baby, so Cleopatra thought about continuing with her nap. After all, the baby's father was right there and would certainly awaken if he was needed. Just then the cat saw something that erased all thoughts of napping. The baby stood up and began to walk, and it was walking toward the pier that jutted out into the pond.

The cat looked over at the still-sleeping father and ran over to him. She grabbed hold of the sleeve of his shirt with her teeth and pulled as hard as she could, trying to wake the man. Still sound asleep, he reached over and tried to brush her away, as he might do to a fly that was bothering him. Cleopatra thought for a moment about giving the man a good hard bite on his bare arm, but she thought better of it when she remembered the unfortunate incident with the mail carrier.

She looked over toward the pier and was shocked by how fast the baby had moved toward the end. Frantically she looked around, at first searching for someone who might be able to help, but she had chosen this place because no one came here. Then she realized she was looking to make sure that no one could see what she was about to do. Finding no one in sight, she called out, "Dear Bastet, Mother of all cats and protector of all who serve you. Please give me the strength and power that only you can give so that your servant can do what needs be done."

Later when people talked about that Special Bowiefest, they would always begin with where they were, whom they were with, and what they were doing. The stories would always start with "I was at the grill with my family, cooking another round of hot dogs" or "I was with my friends and the dads, and we were all playing Keep-Away-Catch-Return with the dogs." Maybe that was a way of trying to explain and understand the things that happened next.

First, an astonishing sound filled the air and seemed to push down on everyone, stopping them all where they were. Every creature with two legs or four froze in place, and some were brave enough to say later that they had felt frozen with fear. It was a sound that most had only heard in the zoo or while watching National Geographic or something on Animal Planet. Maybe they had heard it at the circus or in a Tarzan movie. It certainly was not a sound heard on a beautiful summer day in a nice-sized city in Maryland. As much as no one, especially the adults, wanted to admit that it was true, the sound had been a roar.

Certainly people wanted to be afraid, but there was no time for that. Before anyone else could move, Anthony, The Wilkinsons' huge English Mastiff, let out a howl that filled the park almost as much as the roar. Then almost every animal that was not tied down or locked up began to run toward the pier side of the pond.

Fitzwallace the Falcon, whose hearing was almost as good as his eyesight, was the first to respond. After all the fuss and ceremony at the opening of Bowiefest, his human, David, had decided to rest his arm and put the bird on his perch. Normally a bird like a falcon would have been tethered or tied down, but David knew his bird could not fly and was wearing a hood that prevented him from seeing where he was going, so he had not bothered to secure the leather straps that hung from the bird's legs. This had been a mistake. The crafty falcon had been keeping a secret from David. At the sound of Anthony's call, the falcon swung his head back and forth, trying to pinpoint the direction of the sound. Once he did, David could only watch helplessly as Fitzwallace dipped his head down, reached up with his talons, and tore his beautiful new hood from his head. In less than a second, the falcon took off, something he had not been able to do in two years. He was flying, and he was free.

The Newfoundlands dove into the water the moment they heard Anthony. But they were at the far side of the pond, and it would take them time to swim across.

Andy Anaconda knew he could not join in on the stampede, but this was the perfect time for him to play a joke on his humans. They had bragged about how strong his big, clear tank was. They had said that it would be impossible for the twenty-five-foot snake to break out. They had assured the parents of the smaller pets that all of them would be perfectly safe this year. So it seemed to him that, in the midst of all this confusion of running dogs, this would be the perfect time to show the humans who was really in charge. The huge anaconda wound his beautiful brown, black, tan, and cream coils up until he just touched the sides of the tank. Then, he flexed his muscles and pushed hard and fast against the sides of the tank. The glue that held the walls of the tank together could not withstand the pressure, and water began to rush out all over the ground. The giant snake never did have any intention of escaping. The fun was in watching his humans frantically running around, trying to stop the water and wondering what they would do if he did get loose. Andy smiled peacefully to himself and relaxed. He had a pretty good feeling that this would be the last time he was removed from the comfort of his home tank and put on display for others to point at.

Buda Kali, The Rock, and the other cats watched and laughed at all the commotion. They too had heard the chilling roar followed by The Noble Anthony's howl. Like all cats, they knew The Power of Bastet had created the roar and that The Creature was being released. Whatever was happening, The Creature would take care of it from this point, and all would be as it should be.

The Greyhounds raced to arrive at the pier first. Then they stopped in their tracks and whimpered as a huge wet creature with deep green eyes dragged itself out of the water and back onto the pier. Its mouth held a human baby by the leg. The Creature gently set the dripping child down on the pier and turned its glowing eyes toward the dogs. The new young Greyhound tried to bark to hide his fear. Dowland moved to stop him for fear that it might startle The Creature, but it did not matter. The young dog was so frightened no sound would come out anyway.

Soon the Great Danes arrived. The Greyhounds may have been faster, but the long legs of Sebastian and Julia allowed for longer strides, so they had not been far behind. They too stopped short. The strange animal glared at them, intimidating even these big dogs, and they backed away from it.

Though The Noble Anthony might have been the bravest and most powerful dog at Bowiefest, English Mastiffs were not built for speed, so it was the two mixed-breed mongrels who lived around the corner from The Wilkinsons' that arrived next. Rosie and Poise knew exactly what to do, so they took charge. Rosie and Poise were a mix of about seventeen different breeds, and they seemed to have inherited the intelligence of all of their ancestors. Rosie called out to the dogs already there, "All of you step back and keep away. My Lady is not quite herself right now, and we don't want any of you to get hurt by accident."

"My Lady," Poise called to The Creature. "My Lady, you need to follow me into the woods so we can get you out of sight before the humans arrive."

The Creature turned its head toward the child and then back to Poise.

"Please, My Lady. Trust us to take care of everything. You must come with me and get out of sight RIGHT NOW!" Poise heard a squawk, so she looked up at the sky. Fitzwallace was circling overhead. "My Lady, please, we must go—now."

"My Beloved, go with her." The strong and commanding voice of The Noble Anthony filled the air. The look on The Creature's face softened, and suddenly it seemed less frightening. It looked at Anthony almost as if it were embarrassed that he should see it this way. The beast turned away and quickly, quietly, with its head hung down, followed Poise into the woods. Now all the others could concentrate on the child.

Yes, the child. It was sitting in the grass, starting to realize something had happened to it. It was just beginning to twist up its face to let out a good loud baby scream. Rosie called out to The Mastiff, "Anthony, get the others moving. I know you want to go to her, but my sister, Poise, will take good care of My Lady."

Anthony nodded in agreement with Rosie and called to the Great Danes, "Quick, while I get wet, you cover up the footprints." Then he told the Greyhounds, "As soon as I come out of the water, begin to wake the father." As he turned to enter the water, he saw the Newfoundlands arriving and said, "Good, Scout and Reagan will help you. Hurry, the humans are almost here."

The humans arrived just in time to see dogs running all over the place. As it is with all people, everyone saw something different. Some saw the Greyhounds licking and nudging a sleepy and confused man underneath the big oak tree. Others say they saw Poise and some of the others near some great big shadow of a thing entering the woods. Many were confused by the Great Danes and the younger of the Newfoundlands, who were running around in circles for no apparent reason. Fortunately, most of them saw what they were supposed to see, and that was Anthony and Scout, both good and wet, snuggling with the baby.

Thanks to loving kisses from the dogs, it never did scream or cry. By the time The Wilkinson Family arrived with Scout and Reagan's family, everyone else had already decided what had happened. According to the crowd, the father under the tree had gone to sleep, and his baby had wandered off down the pier and fallen into the water. Scout and Anthony had saved the baby. The crowd told the two families what heroes their dogs were and what wonderful gifts the dogs were to the entire community. Several days later Mayor Robinson would make a speech and give both dogs medals. Of course, the father of what was later found to be a little boy would never again be left alone with his child. His wife would tell people for years that the man could sleep through anything and that she had the most wonderful and perfect little boy, who did not even cry after all he had been through.

Gradually the crowd began to thin out, and the people returned to their tables and grills to begin packing up for the trip home. It had truly been a Bowiefest to remember. There had been that strange roaring sound. What had that been? Then The Wilkinsons' dog, Anthony, had let out that weird howl. Next, every single dog that could had taken off to the pier for no reason that anyone could see. Somehow Scout and Anthony had found and saved the baby boy. On top of all this, the falcon Fitzwallace, whom everyone assumed could not fly, had not only taken off and circled over the pond while everything was going on but then returned to his perch, and he had gone home with his humans. Wow, this Bowiefest would be talked about for years.

⌒⋒⌒

Michelle Wilkinson and The Boys went back to their table to begin packing up their things. Michael stayed by the pier with Anthony, who for some reason seemed reluctant to leave. "What's going on, Big Fellow? We need to get back to the table so we can dry you off some before we leave. This has been a really big day for you." He rubbed the BIG DOG on the head and then gave his side a couple of good pats. "I always knew you were a hero dog. What a good boy you are!"

Then something under one of the bushes glimmered in the late-afternoon sun. The Father walked over to it with Anthony by his side, and when he bent down, he saw the sun reflecting off the lens of a small pair of sunglasses. The glasses were the size that a doll might wear. Beside the glasses was a small straw hat with holes cut in the top for...ears? It was Cleopatra's hat. It could not belong to anyone else. He stood up quickly and looked around. "Cleopatra," he called, and then he looked down at the dog. "Anthony, where is she?"

It was then that he heard barking and looked up to see Rosie and Poise over by the edge of the woods, standing as if they were protecting an entrance. Anthony was already heading in their direction. The big dog looked back at him, letting him know he should follow. Rosie and Poise parted to let Anthony and his human pass. There on the grass under the trees was a completely wet and exhausted Cleopatra.

"What in the world?" It was all The Father could think to say. He bent over to pick up the cat but then realized that he had never touched her before. He wondered if it would be safe. Then Anthony nudged his leg, and the look in his dog's eyes told him it would be all right. Again he found himself saying, "What in the world," as he picked up the limp cat and held her in his arms.

He stepped carefully, trying to handle her as gently as possible, and so he was looking at the ground as he walked. That was the only reason he saw it almost hidden among all the dog prints in the mud. In with all the others was one giant paw print. It was way bigger than Anthony's, and he was the biggest dog around. Strangely, unlike the prints of the other dogs, the paw print had no toenail marks in it. This print looked like that of a cat, whose claws retract and do not show when it walks. No one had a cat anywhere close to the size that would leave a print like this.

The Father looked at the almost unconscious cat in his arms and at her small little wet feet, and then he looked back at the ground. This time he saw the hair. As he studied the ground, he could see more of them. They were long, thick, and golden-brown hairs. They were just like the ones he had seen that first day at Dr. Daisy's office. Again he looked down at the cat in his arms. The Cat that was almost the exact same color as the hairs. He heard a soft "woof," and he looked at Anthony.

"You're right, Big Guy. We'd better get your girl back home before she catches cold."

Back on the paths, The Father was able to move a little faster. Other families with their baskets and coolers were heading toward the various parking areas. He was pleasantly surprised by how many people greeted him. Or maybe they were actually greeting Anthony.

"Hey, Anthony, great job today, big guy. Oh, hi, Michael," Scott, the Boy Scout Leader, said as he approached the *BIG DOG* for a congratulatory pat on the head.

Peter, who lived across the street from The Family, said, "Hi, Mike. Hi, Anthony. Good save today. Hey, Anthony, where's Cleopatra? I'm used to seeing the two of you together."

Then Miles, the former UPS guy, stepped up and said, "There you are, Michael. I'm pretty sure Michelle and the kids are looking for you and Cleopatra. Oh, there she is. Is she OK? Isn't she usually sitting on Anthony's head?"

Mayor Robinson even came over to say, "Anthony! Boy, you and Scout did a great job today."

"Hey, Mr. Wilkinson. Hey, Anthony!" little Rachel, one of the kids from the bus stop, shouted. "Oh, I'd better go and tell Mrs. Wilkinson you've found Cleopatra. She's been really worried about her."

The Father could see his wife coming toward him with a look of concern on her face.

"Oh, please tell me that's Cleopatra you're holding. I've been looking all over for her. Where did you find her?"

"She was in the woods not far from the pier. You know, when all the commotion started, I thought it might have something to do with her. You know sometimes strange things happen when she's around. I don't think so this time. She was kind of hidden in the woods with Rosie and Poise, the dogs from around the corner. At first I thought that maybe one of them had hurt her, but then I realized that they seemed to be standing around her almost like they were guarding or protecting her."

While he spoke, his wife took the cat from him. Since she had no towel or blanket, she grabbed one of the spare shirts she had brought for The Boys and wrapped the wet cat in it.

"How in the world did she get so wet? She won't even go out in the rain without her rain slicker and hat. I would have thought when Anthony howled she would have gone to find him to see what was going on." Suddenly she seemed to realize that none of her questions were going to be answered (or needed to be answered) right then. So instead she called out to The Boys, "Let's get going, guys. I've got to get her home."

Usually when The Family traveled in the van, if Anthony and Cleopatra were with them, The Father would drive, The Mother would hold Cleopatra in her lap, The Boys would sit in the back seat with Anthony, and any gear would be in the back cargo area. That did not happen on the ride home from Bowiefest. This time The Parents were in the front seats, The Boys were in the back seat with all of The Family's picnic gear, and Anthony and Cleopatra were in the cargo area.

When the Father opened the back, the BIG DOG had just jumped in and lain there waiting, until Cleopatra was placed between his two huge arms. He immediately began to lick her head to comfort and dry her. "My Lady, how could you put yourself in danger like that?"

She stretched out and rested her head against one of his legs, letting him continue to attempt to dry her. "I could do no less. You never would have forgiven me, My Love, if I had let harm come to the child." This time she put a paw on his nose to stop the licking because in reality he was actually making her wetter. "The child is safe, and that is all that matters. Were the others able to cover all the tracks?"

"Yes, My Dear. I think so. The Father may have seen something, but I do not think so, and I am sure that he would not associate what he saw with you anyway."

"Then indeed all is well and as it should be."

That night The Family cheered Anthony and Scout when the TV news anchor called them The Hero Dogs of Bowiefest. The Father petted his dog with love and pride, but he could not help but look at the sleeping Cleopatra with her golden-brown coat and just wonder.

Teatime

Everyone at school knew that Gwen Nelson and the Lady Cleopatra had become Special Friends. Formal announcements were never sent out, and heralds never went through the streets proclaiming it. Everyone just knew, because Gwen had told everyone. Most of the children had never even dared to touch The Cat, so for one of them to have My Lady over for tea was something very different and certainly very special. Actually, it was newsworthy.

All the other girls in Gwen's class wanted to know what it was like to have Cleopatra visit her. Did she go by herself? No, The Noble Anthony always brought her. Did Anthony stay and have tea too? Sometimes he did, but sometimes he would return home to be with His Boys. What did they eat? What did they wear? Did they sing songs? Did they dance? Did she let Gwen rub her tummy? The questions went on and on, and Gwen had to admit to herself that SHE LOVED IT. And one tea was going to be the very best one of all because for the first time, her father was going to be home to meet Cleopatra and Anthony.

Mr. Nelson had, of course, heard about the rather strange cat and dog. He had seen them a couple of times on the street. Somehow his work always seemed to keep him away for teatime though, but not that day. That day, he was going to be there for tea, and he was almost as excited about it as his daughter. He had felt it to be a very big honor when his daughter had asked him to help her set the tea table with the tablecloth and the real china cups and saucers that her grandmother had given to her. He had even picked some flowers from the garden to place on the table. Of course, then Gwen had shooed him away while she went and got dressed for the big event. Allen Nelson found his wife reading in the family room. "So when do we get started with all this?" he asked.

"Oh, they should be here any time now." She saw her husband looking out the window and down the street toward The Wilkinsons' house. Both parents knew this move had been harder on their daughter than usual, and they had been very happy that she had found friends, both human and animal. "You know, Allen, maybe this would be a good time for me to fill you in on some things I haven't told you before. Not that they were anything bad. I just wasn't sure that you would believe me. Have a seat." She patted the spot beside her on the couch.

"So what's the big deal? I've seen them on the street. The Big Mastiff with the cat sitting on his head. The cat always seems to have on some kind of silly-looking Egyptian clothing. Some people dress their dogs up, so I guess Michelle Wilkinson has the right to dress up her cat if she wants to."

"Well, there are some other things that are a little stranger than that," his wife explained. "I told you about taking her to the school bus stop that first day and seeing that car almost plow into the kids, right?"

"Sure. It was scary, but the car stopped, and no one was hurt. So no real harm done."

"There have been a couple of other things that I haven't told you about. The first one was a few weeks ago, when Gwen had that fever and had to stay home from school for a couple of days. I was able to use some of my leave time and stay home with her." Her husband nodded. "So she didn't go to school that morning, but that afternoon she had a visitor, kind of. Her visitor was the elder Wilkinson boy, Jeffrey. The Dog was with him but not the cat. I thought something might be wrong because the boy seemed rather uncomfortable about being here." Lynette Nelson could see that her husband wanted to know where all of this was leading.

"Jeffrey told me that his dog, Anthony, knew that Gwen hadn't been at the bus stop and that Anthony wanted to be sure that Gwen and the family were all right."

"What?" The surprised look on Gwen's father's face was no surprise to his wife at all.

"That is exactly the way that he said it. 'Anthony wanted to know.'" She emphasized the dog's name. "I told him that Gwen was sick and would be out of school for a couple of days until she was better. That was when he told me that when something like this happens, I should call his mother and let her know so that she can tell Anthony, The Dog. I laughed at the boy and said, 'Sure, I'll think about it,' but he went on to tell me that all the other parents did this."

"You're kidding," Allen Nelson said in utter amazement.

"No, I'm not. I actually asked some of them, and what I got back was, 'Oh, sure, we all call Michelle to let her know if someone is sick or if we're going to be out of town. Anthony worries about the children and needs to know that they are safe and well.' Reporting to a dog about the well-being of their families did not seem to be strange to any of them."

A look of knowing and surprise suddenly lit up her husband's face. "So that was why you had *ME* call Michelle and tell her when we had to go to your grandmother's birthday party."

"Right. I put it off on you so that I wouldn't feel like I was obeying the wishes of a dog."

Allen sat back and patted his wife's hand a little to reassure her. "OK, honey, that was a little different, but doesn't it make you feel good to know that all of us are part of a good and caring community of people who look out for each other and our little girl?"

"Yes, all that part is good, but there's more. On the day before the first of these tea parties, I came home from work, and there was this gigantic box sitting right here on the couch where you're sitting now. There was no postage or shipping information on it, and I knew that I hadn't ordered or bought anything. There was just a note taped to the top that said, 'Thought that you might need this tomorrow. If you have any questions, call Michelle Wilkinson. Love, Auntie Emma-Gene.'" Lynette Nelson paused to give her husband a moment for everything to sink in.

"The house was locked? What was in the box? Who the heck is this Auntie Emma-Gene person?" Allen Nelson's voice got more excited and a little angrier with every question.

"I thought that those might be your questions," his wife replied. "Yes, my dear, the house was locked. We live in a good neighborhood, but we're not stupid. The box contained a humongous straw hat with horrendous flowers all over it and a necklace big enough for Gwen to jump rope with if she wanted to. It also had a feather boa and…I guess I'll call them lace arm bands because they weren't gloves. It's all completely hilarious looking, and if The Big Mastiff decides to join in with the tea today, you'll see him wearing all of it." She looked over at her husband and then added, "Honey, you should close your mouth now before you start to drool."

"So did you call Michelle? What did she say, and who is this Emma-Gene person?"

"Of course, I called Michelle. I told her what was in the box, and she laughed, saying that it was for Anthony to wear if he wanted to stay for the tea. She said that this Auntie Emma-Gene was the one who makes all of Cleopatra's outfits and also all the gowns, special dresses, and outfits for half the county. So then I asked her how the woman managed to get into our very locked house, and she really did laugh out loud and said to just get used to it. She told me that we were now official members of the community.

"Allen Nelson was shaking his head. "I know why you didn't tell me any of this: because you are right; I don't think that I would have believed you. I've never heard anything like this before. Maybe we should—"

The squealing of a little girl running down the stairs cut him off.

"They're here. They're here. Come on, Daddy. They're here." Neither parent had heard a knock or a ringing doorbell.

"Allen, she's happy." That was all his wife could say to him as he headed toward the door.

Mr. Nelson met his daughter at the front door. He was not surprised that Gwen had changed from the usual jeans and T-shirt to a pretty pink dress, but the big floppy hat with flowers—and, of course, the feathered boa—did take him back just a little. What surprised him most, though, was the quick look of inspection she gave him, followed by a look that said, "I guess that will have to do." The giggles had left her, and the young girl straightened her back, smoothed out her dress with her hands, took a deep breath, and opened the door.

"Welcome to our home, My Lady. It is so nice that you and The Noble Anthony are able to join us today."

Allen Nelson watched in amazement as his daughter performed what might be called a curtsy, or at least a bend of the knees.

When the door opened, Mr. Nelson very quickly discovered that seeing this pair as he drove down the street did not at all compare to the experience of viewing them up close and personal. The massive dog filled the open door, and Gwen's father found himself looking into the most trusting eyes he had ever seen. Of course, the cat was sitting on the dog's head, but this time her outfit echoed his daughter's, with hat, necklace, and feathered boa.

It was a lot to take in at one time. He felt his daughter poke him in the side of the leg. "Yes, welcome, and please come in," he said invitingly. He watched in amazement as The Noble Anthony and The Lady Cleopatra entered The Nelson home as one complete unit.

"And will The Noble Anthony be joining us today for tea?" Gwen asked. Her father did not hear any kind of response, and yet, he could not misread the look of delight that appeared on his daughter's face. It told him that there had indeed been some kind of answer.

"How very nice! My mother is here to give you any assistance that you might need."

Allen had no idea when his wife had arrived to stand beside him, but there she was. Lynette turned and gestured upstairs, toward Gwen's room, as if she had been given instructions to point the way. Allen Nelson could do nothing else but follow the parade of cat, dog, daughter, and wife up the stairs.

Once there, he opened the connection on the laptop so that his daughter's best friend, Athena, who, of course, was also dressed for the day, could join in. The cat jumped down from the dog's head and took a seat on one of the small chairs around the tea table while Gwen's mother began to dress the dog. Anthony, of course, sat like a complete gentleman while she fastened the necklace around his neck and draped the feathered boa over his shoulders. He then lifted his huge front paws one at a time so she could slide the lace bands, which were passing for gloves, on his front legs. Finally, he ducked his head slightly so that she could place the monstrous flowered hat on his head. Even though the huge Mastiff was dressed in such a ridiculous outfit, he somehow still remained very much The Noble Anthony.

Plates on the table held assorted cookies for humans, dogs, and cats, and, of course, Gwen, playing "Mother," would be in charge of pouring the tea. As the adults backed out of the room and closed the door, the immediate sounds of fun, laughter, and giggles filled the air, including one rather strange, very deep laugh.

The laughing, giggling, storytelling, and singing had been going on for almost an hour when Gwen finally got her nerve up. "You know, My Lady,

Athena and I have been thinking about something that we thought would be a great idea and great fun." Gwen paused for a moment to watch the cat's reaction. Seeing none and getting a quick nod from the girl on the laptop screen beside her, she went on, "Some of the girls at school think that it's nice that you and I and Athena have these tea parties together, but they also feel a little left out." Again she paused and waited. "So, we were thinking that maybe one day we should all have A Great Big Tea Party and invite everyone from school. Wouldn't that be fun?" Her voice had now bubbled over into excitement. Unfortunately, the response was silence.

Athena chose this moment to join in. "Yes, yes, it would be great. I could have all my friends here too on their laptops. Our parents could put all the pictures and movies on social media for the whole world to see, and WE COULD GO VIRAL!"

Even louder silence.

Finally, Anthony said, "I do not believe that this is something that My Lady would enjoy taking part in."

"Why not? Why not?" asked both the little girls. "It will be so much fun... and we want to. We really, really want to," they pleaded, with desire and delight in their voices. Cleopatra put her paw down softly onto the table, and all the talking stopped. She turned to Anthony and gave him a nod. The BIG DOG spoke again.

"Gwen, you and Athena have a very special friendship with My Lady, but it would no longer be special if it was shared with everyone. Maybe even some of your school friends have already seen too much. Friendship is something that is very special. It is the giving and receiving of trust. It is something to be treasured and to be respected. It is not something to be exploited to show off one's own popularity. Friendship is the silent and invisible badge of honor that someone has entrusted you with the special gift of themselves."

Both girls were quiet, and they perhaps felt a little ashamed. It was Cleopatra who knew to change the subject. "Oh, look, My Lovelies, I think that we each have time for one more cookie before My Beloved and I must leave."

Allen and Lynette Nelson were waiting for them at the door when they all came downstairs, even though no one had told them that the party was over. Mrs. Nelson removed Anthony's wardrobe and placed everything back in the box from Auntie Emma-Gene so it would all be ready for the next tea party. As the dog and cat were about to leave, Gwen turned to her parents and said, "The Noble Anthony and His Lady Cleopatra would like to thank you both for providing this delightful time for us to spend together."

To the complete dismay of her husband, Lynette Nelson replied, "It was our privilege and honor to serve you."

After their guests left, Lynette asked her daughter, "So, are we going to have the full-blown tea party with everyone that you and Athena have ever known?"

Gwen was a little quiet, and her mother could hear the disappointment in her daughter's voice when she said, "It seemed like a good idea that might be fun, but after talking it over, we all thought better of it. We have decided not to do it. We didn't want to exploit our friendship by showing off and bragging about it, because *'friendship is the silent and invisible badge of honor that someone has entrusted you with the special gift of themselves.'*"

Then she stood up straight and looked directly at both her parents. For just the briefest moment, Mr. and Mrs. Nelson saw their daughter not as her ten-year-old self, but as the twenty-five-year-old strong and confident woman she would be one day. Then ten-year-old Gwen returned and said, "I'm going to go back upstairs and put everything away now." And she was gone.

Allen looked at his wife in complete disbelief of what he had just heard and seen.

His wife only looked back at him and said, "Yes, this kind of thing has been going on ever since the dog and cat showed up that morning with the rest of the kids."

"So what you're telling me is that our daughter is learning about life, relationships, honor, and trust from a dog and a dressed-up cat?"

Lynette Nelson nodded, leaned over, and gave her husband a quick kiss on his cheek. "Allen, you know that old saying that we hear all the time about how it takes a village to raise a child?"

"Sure. Of course. What about it?"

"Well, no one has ever said that everyone in the village helping to raise the child has to be human."

Mr. Nelson flopped down on the couch, completely befuddled. A village teaching a child about life, yes, that he could understand, but a dog and a cat?

The Bell Tolls for Thee

It was a Friday—the kind of Friday that almost never happens during the school year, except as part of Thanksgiving, Winter, or Spring vacations. This Friday was the beginning of a *FOUR-DAY WEEKEND*. A statewide teacher's conference was taking place on Friday, and there was a federal holiday on Monday, and that would mean *FOUR DAYS* home from school.

The Boys were so thrilled they could hardly contain themselves. Bobby was especially excited because since he was only seven, he had not experienced many special events like this one—four days to play with his friends, to watch TV, or to play video games. That, of course, also meant four whole days to do the extra homework his teachers had assigned and four days to clean his side of the bedroom that he shared with Jeffrey. Still, it was a glorious time for all involved—all except Cleopatra.

To no one's surprise, The Wilkinsons had discovered their cat despised any changes in her environment or schedule. She did not like for the furniture to be moved or rearranged, and she certainly did not like for the schedule of The Family's life to change in any way. After all, there had to be some standard to live by. Monday through Friday, The Boys got up, ate breakfast, and went to school at the same time. They came home, did their homework, had dinner, played some, and went to bed. Weekends were, of course, different. That was allowed. There were, of course, scheduled school holidays and breaks and the scheduled summer vacation. This had all been set forth by the school, given to all the parents at the beginning of the school year, and posted on the refrigerator of each and every home for all to see, as it should be.

Somehow this particular four-day event had been missed on the usual posting of holidays, and the school had just sent out an announcement letter to the parents, explaining the additional day off and hoping that no one would be inconvenienced by the mistake. Silly humans; not one had thought to send Cleopatra her own personal letter, and she was INDEED inconvenienced by the mistake. Though no one actually understood why. This meant that she was not a happy and loving cat when Anthony arrived to get her from her bed in the linen closet that morning.

"Why are you getting me up? There is no place to go. We do not have to take The Children to the bus stop." Her grumpiness continued when The Mother put out a new can of Le Kit-tay Cat Food. This time The Cat showed her displeasure by trying to bury the can of food before it was even opened. The Lady was so fussy about her wardrobe selection for the day that The Mother finally gave up and left Cleopatra sitting in nothing but her gold hoop earrings, her leg bands, and her emerald ring, and that had never happened before. Even The Father, who had been taking slightly more interest in Cleopatra since Bowiefest, while keeping his distance, also found himself caught up in The Day of Her Displeasure.

Though The Boys might have the day off from school, Michael Wilkinson still had to go to his office. All the commotion over Cleopatra's mood was disturbing his morning routine. So trying to be a good human father, when he saw her walking close beside him, he thought he would try to help. It was an innocent enough gesture. The Father simply reached down and stroked the cat on the top of the head with his fingers and said, "What's the matter, old girl? Not having a great day?"

Green eyes flashed, and Cleopatra moved just that little bit closer to him, just ever so slightly brushing herself against the leg of his suit, depositing just one hair onto that dark, navy-blue suit. Just one golden-brown hair.

Cleopatra knew that she was not an *OLD GIRL* she was *AGELESS*. And later that day, The Father would learn that lesson.

Just as Cleopatra was glowering at The Father, Bobby went charging by. "I know what to do. I know how to make Cleopatra happy again." And off he went, running into the laundry room. "I'll get her string. That will do it. Her string always makes her happy."

From different parts of the house, the different family members warned, "No. *No*. No, no, no!" But it was too late. Bobby had grabbed one of the beautiful entertainment pieces that Auntie Emma-Gene had made for Cleopatra. It was four feet of shiny gold sparkly ribbon attached to a two-foot stick that a person could shake and drag across the floor. What the rest of The Family knew that seven-year-old Bobby did not was that the shiny gold sparkly ribbon did not make Cleopatra happy. The shiny gold sparkly ribbon made Cleopatra *CRAZY*!

Though it was rarely spoken of in polite conversation, Cleopatra was a cat. Cats are sight driven in that they respond to things that move. To a cat, four feet of shiny gold sparkly ribbon dragged across the floor or waved in the air is something that must be *chased* and caught and then chased and caught some more.

There is no speed like that of a seven-year-old boy who is happily doing something for his family and his pet, so there was no stopping Bobby. Cleopatra came out of nowhere and made a flying leap at the ribbons while delicately springing off the wall. Great-Grandmother Wilkinson's picture could be rehung later. Bobby took the ribbons down low, pulling them across the floor. The Cat turned in midair, coming down with the ribbons and knocking The Father's cell phone off the table. It bounced against the wall before splashing into the fish tank. Fortunately, The Father had been looking for an excuse to buy a new one anyway.

The Mother came into the room with an unfortunate cup of coffee in her hand to try to stop things, just in time to feel two back feet spring off her chest. Warm, wet coffee dribbled down the front of her nice, clean T-shirt. She would have to change her clothes. Jeffrey walked by just in time to catch a half-eaten bowl of cereal that was careening off the table. All the while, Bobby was still yelling, "Be happy, Cleopatra. Be happy, Cleopatra!"

Anthony called out, "My Lady, what has come over you?"

A strange mixture of golden-brown hair and green eyes, entangled in shiny gold sparkly ribbon, came rolling by. "I cannot help myself. Make him stop. Make him stop!"

"Come on, Cleopatra. Be happy now," squealed Bobby as he continued his run.

"Anthony, make him stop!" The Cat pleaded again.

"Michelle, do something!" The Father yelled, catching hold of the TV remote as it went flying by. "Another go 'round and we'll be living in a tent in the backyard."

"My Lady, please control yourself," The Mastiff asked as a water bowl landed on top of his head, and The Not So Noble Anthony found himself very wet, with water running down his face.

"Did I not tell you that I cannot? Someone please take that thing from The Boy," a very desperate Cleopatra yelled out as she raced past, following the shiny gold sparkly ribbon across the floor.

In the end, it was Jeffrey who sacrificed himself and put an end to the madness. Poor Jeffrey, who happened to be standing in the right place at the wrong time. Cleopatra made one more flying leap into the air after the magical shiny gold sparkly ribbon, and this time she sank her claws deep into the tangled mess. Jeffrey simply reached up and caught Cleopatra in midair, bringing the crazed cat, four feet of shiny gold sparkly ribbon, and two feet of golden stick all down on top of himself.

At first Cleopatra was relieved. Both she and the shiny gold sparkly ribbon had finally stopped moving. Then she realized that the reason she had stopped moving was that one of The Boys was touching and holding her, and she was wrapped in the newly formed cocoon of shiny gold sparkly ribbon

"AREEEEREEEEMEEEE!" The cat screeched out at him.

Jeffrey, in shock and surprise, did what anyone who was holding a cat that made that sound would do: he immediately dropped her ungraciously onto the floor. Tangled in all the ribbon, Cleopatra did not have a chance to gather herself into her usual gracious and perfect landing. With her legs caught up in it, she just went *SPLAT* on the floor, landing hard on her stomach.

Completely forgetting that she was the one causing all the noise and confusion in the house, she turned her anger onto The Boys. "*I will not have this*! I will not be treated this way! If you BOYS want to run around and make a lot of noise for no reason at all and act like a gaggle of noisy geese, then it is geese you shall be!"

The house was quiet. No one moved. No one made a sound. Only The Mother, The Boys, and Anthony had heard the voice. The Father had stopped because the others had, and he did not want them to know that he had no idea what was going on. They all knew that something was about to happen to one or all of them. It was just a matter of how horrifying the something was going to be. They were all just waiting. And waiting. And waiting. Nothing happened. Neither The Boys nor anyone else had turned into geese or anything else. So then they all turned to look at Cleopatra, who was still standing on the floor in front of Jeffrey. Still nothing happened. They all looked at Jeffrey. Poor Jeffrey was completely entangled in shiny gold sparkly ribbon with a stick pointing out. Although Jeffrey looked ridiculous, no one had become a goose. There was not one goose in the house, anywhere. This meant that there was only one thing to do, and that is exactly what The Family did. They laughed.

The entire Human Family laughed at Cleopatra. The Noble Anthony, however, did not laugh at His Beloved Lady, because Anthony knew that His Lady was feeling embarrassed. She had been out of control chasing the shiny gold sparkly ribbon, and she had not been able to turn The Boys into geese, though that part he was rather happy about. And worst of all, she had been laughed at. The Big Mastiff watched as Cleopatra walked into the laundry room and then slipped outside through The Puppy Door. She was alone, and she was on the ground. An embarrassed Cleopatra could be a dangerous Cleopatra.

⌒⌒⌒

The Watsons lived up the street from The Wilkinson Family. They were a very nice older couple. When it snowed or when the leaves needed raking, The Father would take His Boys over to their house to help. There would always be homemade cookies and hot chocolate for their kind deed. Mrs. Watson kept a beautiful garden, and all through the spring, summer, and fall, she would share what she liked to call The Overflow Garden with her neighbors. Mr. Watson was a little hard of hearing and could never seem to hear the doorbell ring, so to let him know when someone was coming near his house, Mrs. Watson kept Geraldine The Goose.

Geese were wonderful guard animals. In fact, several branches of the US Military used them to guard and protect their outposts. Geese are very territorial, and they do not like anyone new in what they see as *their* territory. Sometimes they do not even want someone whom they knew to enter their territory. Normally, Geraldine would have been out and about patrolling her backyard against all possible intruders, but for the past two weeks, the big white goose with the amazingly loud *HONK, HONK, HONK* had been distracted by a higher calling. Much to everyone's delight and surprise, Geraldine had presented her humans with two wonderful yellow goslings.

She was a wonderful goose mother who knew all about how to take care of her babies as well as how to protect her human family. She did not know anything about school schedules or long four-day weekends. The goose did not know that Cleopatra's morning had not begun well. The new mother did not know that Cleopatra had been embarrassed by her own behavior with the shiny gold sparkly ribbons or that the cat was angry because The Boys had not turned into geese when she had wanted them to. The goose only knew that it was a beautiful day and time to take her two goslings out for a walk in the backyard for the very first time. Geraldine also did not know that an upset cat was heading straight into her backyard to visit The Forbidden Catnip Patch.

Although the people in Bowie knew Mrs. Watson for The Overflow Garden, her wonderful cookies, and her hot chocolate, every cat in the county knew her for The Catnip Patch. What had begun as one little plant many years ago was now a monster hedge, towering six feet tall and ten feet across in the back corner of The Watsons' garden. The vines and leaves wrapped around and intertwined with each other in ropes so thick and heavy it was impossible to see through the mass. Some branches were so thick that, when cut, they actually showed the rings of their years of life, as a tree does. Old leaves and new leaves mixed to make a soft and alluring dark-green bed on the ground. Any pressure from a stray paw would release the overwhelming magical, powerful, hypnotic scent that few cats could resist. It was rumored that The Patch could actually purr to lure unsuspecting cats into its depths. Some of these cats were never seen or heard of again.

Like all of the cats in the neighborhood, Cleopatra had been forbidden from entering The Patch. Mrs. Watson had requested that the cat stay away because she did not enjoy golden-brown hairs stuck all over her catnip when she made her catnip tea, catnip salad, catnip and turnip soup, and the family favorite of every holiday, catnip and green bean casserole. This morning, Cleopatra did not care about any silly rules or requests. She needed comfort, and the wind was blowing in the right direction to waft the alluring scent right past her. Yes, a good long wallow in the sweet green magical leaves might go a long way toward making her forget the horrible morning.

The Patch was particularly wonderful that morning. The early sun warmed its leaves just enough to make a perfectly inviting bed. Cleopatra lay on her back and wallowed in the splendor of it all. She was having wonderful dreams of her life in The Temple of Bastet as she embraced her catnip-induced stupor. All was wonderful and as it should be, and then she heard, "HONK, HONK, HONK." What in the world was it? It sounded like geese. How could that be? There were never any geese allowed into The Temple. She decided to ignore them. What did it matter? She was away from The Boys. It was quiet. No, it was not quiet anymore because some goose kept making that horrible "HONK, HONK, HONK" honking noise.

A green eye opened just in time to see two fat and fluffy yellow baby geese walk by. "THE BOYS were geese after all," she thought with much satisfaction. With a smile on her face, Cleopatra lay back into her catnip bed. It had taken a little time, but her spell had worked after all, and that would fix them. That would show those silly, noisy boys not to laugh at her. They would think twice about tormenting her with the shiny golden sparkly thing and touching her without her permission. Just wait until Anthony saw his boys now.

Anthony!

HIS BOYS!

Cleopatra jumped straight up, twisted herself in midair, and landed on all four feet. Then she gave herself a complete tip-of-nose-to-tip-of-tail shake as if she had just gotten out of the bathtub. So it had worked. There had been some kind of delay, but she had managed to turn The Boys into geese. Anthony's Boys were now geese. The Noble Mastiff would not be pleased. Not at all. Well, if she had turned them into geese, she could most certainly turn them back into Boys. It was easy. All she had to say was "You have learned your lesson well, so good, quiet boys you will once again be."

Nothing happened, but The Big White Goose kept "HONK, HONK, HONKing," and it did make it hard to concentrate.

"You do not have to be geese anymore. You may turn back into boys."

Nothing but "HONK, HONK, *HONK.*"

"Please, please, please turn back into boys before The Noble Anthony sees you like this and becomes very displeased with me." The frantic cat begged.

"HONK, HONK, HONK"; the sounds not only continued but also seemed to be growing louder, if that were at all possible.

"I cannot work or think with all that noise going on," Cleopatra said while covering her ears to shield that from the horrible racket. "I will take them home. In the peace and quiet of the house, I will be able to concentrate and change them back. Let me gather them together and take them home."

Mrs. Watson was in one of her upstairs bedrooms. Geraldine could be a very noisy goose, but this amount of noise was a bit much even for her. What in the world was going on out there? She went over to the window that looked down into the backyard. She did not believe what she saw. It was The Wilkinsons' cat. She was sure it was Cleopatra even though the cat was not wearing her usual clothes. The cat had crouched down and seemed to be trying to get the baby geese to go in one direction. No wonder Geraldine was making so much noise. Cleopatra was HUNTING HER BABIES!

Mrs. Watson ran to the telephone. "Michelle. Michelle, you have to do something right away. I'm standing here looking out the window into my backyard, and your cat Cleopatra is hunting Geraldine's new baby geese. Quick, Michelle, you have to come and stop her before something horrible happens."

"Mrs. Watson, I don't think that Cleopatra would do that. She has never shown any signs of hunting anything. I think that it would be much too messy for her. Are you sure that it's Cleopatra?"

"Of course, I'm sure. Just because I'm old and wear glasses doesn't mean I'm blind, you know. You must come right away or send The Boys. She already has them heading toward the sidewalk. Geraldine is right behind them, and she's having a fit. Michelle, please hurry."

The Mother hung up the phone, and as she did, she could hear Geraldine's honking away about something. Well, she would try to be a good neighbor. "Boys, run outside and see what the Watsons' goose is carrying on about, will you? Mrs. Watson seems to think that Cleopatra is hunting Geraldine's new babies. Rescue them if you have to and take them back home, please."

The Boys quickly headed into the laundry room to go out the Puppy Door, which had become their favorite way to enter and exit the house. Even before they made it outside, they could hear the honking Geraldine, and they hurried through the backyard toward the sidewalk.

"Jeffrey, do you really think that Cleopatra is trying to kill the baby geese?"

Bobby asked his older brother, with sadness in his eyes. The younger boy did not want to think of his cat, the cat that he was a little afraid of, hurting other things.

"Are you kidding? Cleopatra doesn't even like to get her feet wet when it rains or when there's dew on the grass. I can't imagine her doing something that would get blood and guts all over herself and her clothes. She'd rather turn the babies into goldfish or something."

Both boys laughed, but as they reached the sidewalk and looked up the street toward the Watson house, they stopped in their tracks.

There she was. Cleopatra was hunched down in a herding, stalking crouch behind the yellow baby geese, moving them right toward The Boys. Behind her was the very upset Geraldine, beating her wings and trying to grab The Cat's tail with her beak. Once she actually caught the tail and tried to pull The Cat away, but Cleopatra quickly flashed her green eyes, momentarily blinding and confusing the big goose so that she dropped The Cat's tail. This allowed Cleopatra to continue herding the babies toward The Wilkinsons' house.

The Boys looked at each other in horror and then rushed toward the geese. "Stop, Cleopatra! Leave them alone!" Jeffrey bravely shouted at the cat.

Cleopatra stopped but only because hearing her name surprised her. Then she looked from The Boys to the yellow babies and just sat down on the sidewalk, realizing that her spell had not worked after all. The Boys were still boys. She was a combination of relieved and disappointed. Of course, once she saw the cat sitting still, Geraldine seized the moment and gave her a good bite on the back of the neck for taking her babies.

Each boy picked up a little yellow ball of fluff and headed toward the Watsons' backyard. Geraldine followed, but this time she was quiet, seeming to understand that her children were safe. The Boys put the babies back into their hutch, and their mother joined them quickly, spreading out her wings, pulling them to her, and sitting on them. The Boys could almost hear the goose's sigh of relief when she knew for sure that her babies were safe.

⚶

All families have their own little traditions and routines. In The Wilkinson household, The Parents would always take a little quiet time for themselves when The Father got home from work. The Boys would greet him with hugs and kisses, but then they would go off to do homework, play, or get a snack with milk and a piece of fruit or a couple of cookies. The Boys knew they would each have time with their father a little later. The Parents told The Boys the adults needed a little time alone to share their day with each other. The Boys called this "My Day Was Worse Than Your Day" time.

Depending on the day, there might be milk and cookies or a glass of wine for The Parents. That day was definitely a glass-of-wine day.

"Where's Anthony?" The Father asked. "He wasn't with The Boys when I came in. Is everything OK?"

"He's upstairs with Cleopatra right now. It's been a rather rough day here."

The Father took the opportunity of The Mother's pause to quickly jump into the story of HIS day. "You know this morning before everything went crazy with Bobby and the cat toy?" He didn't wait for an answer but quickly continued. "You know I usually try to stay away from The Cat in the morning so I don't get any of her hair on my clothes, but this morning, I petted her on the top of the head to try to make her feel better. I remember that she just barely brushed up against me. I didn't think anything of it. Today was my big presentation to the new clients, so my mind was elsewhere. So I was in my office, and everything was all ready. My assistant, Barbara, stuck her head into my office to let me know it was time to go into the meeting, and she screamed out loud, 'Oh my goodness! What's happened to you?'

"Michelle, you are not going to believe this, but I looked down at my suit, and I wasn't wearing a suit anymore. I was wearing a fur coat." The Father watched his wife's eyes get big and her hand cover her mouth, and he wasn't sure if she was trying to hold back a laugh or a scream.

"I was completely covered in hair that looked just like Cleopatra's. I looked like Bigfoot, only without the really big feet." Now he knew for sure that she was trying to hide a laugh. "I automatically reached down to somehow brush it away, and with one push of my hands, it was gone." Now his wife's giggles were beginning to escape. "I'm not kidding. They all just disappeared, just like that. Barbara was shocked, and she kept stammering something about how she must have been wrong, but she wasn't. I don't know how she did it, but I know that it was That Cat. She somehow knows that I didn't want her, and she hates me for it."

There was no longer any holding it back. Michelle Wilkinson grabbed her sides and laughed aloud. "Oh, you poor thing," she finally managed to say. "You did have such a horrible day."

Her husband leaned back, looking at her with annoyance, knowing that he was being mocked. "OK, so tell me. What was so bad about your day?"

Trying hard not to laugh, The Mother sat up straight and looked her husband right in the eye. "I had to put a bell on Cleopatra."

"OK, you win."

It was all that he could say. Michelle Wilkinson sat at her kitchen table and told her husband about Mrs. Watson's call saying that Cleopatra was hunting Geraldine's new babies. She explained that she had sent The Boys to rescue them just in case.

"So what did The Boys say? Was she hunting them?"

"I still don't think so. It's just not like her. It's going to sound crazy to you, but I think she was trying to bring them home."

"You're kidding," The Father said. "Why would she do that? Bring them here?"

"Because this morning when we all laughed at her, she tried to turn The Boys into geese, and it didn't work. When she saw Geraldine's babies, I think that she thought they were The Boys, and she was trying to bring them home before Anthony found out."

The Father just sat and said nothing. He had grown somewhat accustomed to his wife seeming to believe that she could communicate with the pets, but this was stretching his limits.

Michelle just looked back at him, knowing that he did not believe what she was saying. So she went on, "Even after the babies were OK, Mrs. Watson was still upset. She pretty much demanded that Cleopatra should wear a bell so that her geese can hear the cat coming and run away. I wanted to be a good neighbor and keep peace in the neighborhood. So when I tried to get Cleopatra to eat something, I slipped a collar with a bell on it over her head. As soon as she heard it, she looked at me as if I had slapped her in the face, and she ran upstairs. She's been hiding under Jeffrey's bed ever since.

Anthony's been up there with her, but it doesn't look like even he can get her to come out."

Even though The Father had no real understanding of most of what his wife was saying, he did know one thing for sure: His Wife was unhappy. So Michael Wilkinson fell back on what all husbands do when they have no idea what is going on or why their wives are unhappy. He took her hand in his, looked into her eyes, and said, "It will be all right, Honey. Together we'll think of something."

⌒⌒⌒

The Noble Anthony did not look so noble right now. He was lying on the floor of The Boys' room with his head under Jeffrey's bed. It was the only part of him that would fit. Under His Boys' bed was an entire universe of forgotten toys, game and toy parts, lost socks, gloves, and dust bunnies the size of small dogs.

"Please, My Lovely. Please come out."

He coughed from the dust and tried to push an old broken fire engine out of the way so that he could at least see The Lady. "Please come out. This place cannot be healthy for you." He coughed again. "This place certainly cannot be healthy for me."

Cleopatra was at the far corner under the head of the bed, as far away as she could possibly be. She was trying her best not to move because every time that she did, the bell around her neck would make that horrible noise. "Go away and leave me alone. I look hideous with this horrible thing on me, and it keeps making this terrible sound. I cannot believe that The Mother would do this to me and for no reason at all."

"Cleopatra." Anthony almost never called her that. "You know as well as I do that you could never look or be hideous to me, so you must stop saying that. You also know why The Mother put the bell on you, and you know that it was your own fault."

Green eyes flashed, and she lifted her head, but the movement made the bell ring again, and she quickly crouched back down and became still.

"How dare you, Anthony?" The anger was plain in her voice. "Are you saying that I did this to myself?"

"Well, My Lovely, yes. You did do this to yourself. You allowed yourself to lose your temper, and then you completely lost control of yourself. Then you tried to turn My Boys into geese. Thanks to Bastet, it did not work. Then you went off to The Forbidden Catnip Patch, and you know the reasons The Mother has asked you not to go there. If you had not been there, Mrs. Watson would not have thought you were trying to hunt Geraldine's babies, even though you thought they were My Boys. So I have to say yes, My Dearest, you have brought most of this upon yourself. Of course, it does not mean I love you any less. You have always been and will always be My Beloved Lady, and I'm sure that The Mother feels terrible about what she did to you."

The cat was silent. It was the kind of silence that seemed to go on forever. When she finally spoke, she was almost in tears. "But the bell. Did The Mother have to put a bell on me? I was not that bad. The Boys were never actually geese. You know in The Temple, only big, fat, ugly cattle wore bells. They were so dim whited that they could not talk and could hardly think. *I am not cattle! I DO NOT DESERVE THIS!*"

"The Mother did not know about the cattle." Anthony tried to make his voice calming and reassuring. "She did not know what the bell would mean to you. She was only trying to find a way to protect the geese from you and to appease Mrs. Watson. Now, if you come out from under the bed, I will try to take the bell off you."

Cleopatra began to move as slowly as she could so the bell would make as little noise as possible. Finally she made her way through all the rubble and cleared the bed. She immediately threw her body at Anthony so that she could rub herself against him. Feeling the security of The Big Mastiff next to her, the cat suddenly did not care how much noise the bell made.

"My Anthony, I am so very sorry. You know that I would have never hurt Your Boys. I just—"

"I know, My Beloved, but there are always consequences for the things that we say or do. When we do good things, the consequences for us are good, but when we do mean or unkind things…well, I think that you now know the rest." He rubbed his face against hers, marking her as his own. He knew that everything was all right when he heard her purr the Special Purr that she only did for him. "Now put your head down, and let me try to get this horrid thing off you."

She bent her head down as far as she could, and with the very first try, Anthony snagged the elastic collar with his tooth and pulled it over her head. It dropped onto the floor, and Cleopatra quickly knocked it back under the bed as far as it would go. Given how Jeffrey vacuumed the room, there was a very good chance the bell would not be seen again until after he went off to college.

"I must go and talk to The Mother. I know that she was very upset." Cleopatra sighed with resignation. Anthony smiled with pride at His Lady. "We will go see her together."

The Mother was sitting on the couch in the family room, looking very unhappy, but that changed quickly when Cleopatra, seeming to appear out of nowhere, suddenly jumped into her lap.

"Oh, My Lady, I am so sorry that I did that to you. I never should have listened to Mrs. Watson. I should have known you would never hunt the baby geese or anything else. I should have stood up for you. Please forgive me."

Cleopatra stood up and put her front paws on The Mother's shoulders so that she could rub her face against the woman's and mark The Mother as her own. They both closed their eyes and enjoyed the embrace as The Mother put her arms around the cat and stroked her head and back. Cleopatra purred, and they both were content. Soon the cat lay down and rolled over, giving The Mother her tummy, knowing that they could both use the soothing of a good, long, and gentle tummy rub.

Anthony had gone to stand by The Father, who was in the kitchen watching his wife and the cat. He reached down and gave his BIG DOG a good pat on the head. Then he bent down and whispered into The Dog's ear, "I still have no idea what's going on here, but I want to thank you for making both our girls happy again."

The Breaking of the Ice

Whether or not people think the city or town they live in gets a lot of snow in the winter all depends on what they are used to. For those who grew up in Tampa, Florida, and now live in Bowie, Maryland, six inches of snow may seem like a lot of snow. For those who used to live in Bozeman, Montana, and recently moved to Bowie, six inches of snow was hardly even worth talking about. Now the weather people on all the TV stations were saying that The City of Bowie was about to be covered in *thirty-seven* inches OF SNOW! Well, that is a lot of snow for Bowie, and it was worth talking about, a lot.

Everyone was excited about *The Big Snow*, even the adults. Schools were going to be closed. Most businesses were going to be closed. The Federal and local governments would all be closed. They would all hunker down to enjoy the snow, but first they had to get ready. This was when Michael Wilkinson was in his glory. The Father loved plans and lists. The Family had a plan and a list of what to do if a fire started in the house and they had practiced. The Family had a plan and a list of what to do if someone broke into the house and they had practiced. So even though The Family had never practiced it, because no one ever thought it would happen, The Father had secretly been working on a plan and its accompanying list for years in case they ever got more than thirty-six inches of snow. Michael Wilkinson and his family would be ready and prepared. And they were ready.

The night the snow began to fall, The Family sat on the porch together and listened to the silence of the falling snow while drinking hot chocolate. Both cars were parked in the driveway so that they would not block the path of the snowplows. Also there was no longer any room for them in the garage. It seemed that while their van was left unsupervised at the local home-goods store, a brand-new snowblower and generator had managed to sneak into it, and they came home with The Father. Now they were in The Family's garage and were refusing to leave. These items also got to keep company with the four tanks of gas for the grill so that they could cook (in case the power went out) and two full cords of firewood for the fireplace so that they would have heat in at least one room of the house (in case the power went out). There was enough extra gasoline for the generator to supply the power for a nighttime baseball game and for the snowblower to clear a glacier of respectable size and, of course, twelve cases of bottled water, because it was on sale.

Cleopatra did not care for the snow. Snow was cold. Snow was wet. She was a cat. Even though a beautiful emerald-green coat, hat, and boots had arrived by Mysterious Messenger from Auntie Emma-Gene, Cleopatra had decided to let Anthony enjoy the cold, wet, white stuff with The Family on the porch while she enjoyed the warmth and quiet of the fireplace in the family room. All was as it should be as the snow began to cover the city.

In the morning, the entire city awoke to a beautiful bright-blue and sunny sky without a cloud in sight anywhere. It was cold. Very cold. The temperature was in the low teens, but still the comforting hum of snowblowers could be heard everywhere. In fact The Father had talked to some of the other families about his plan for organizing the snow removal. All the equipment was split into groups of large snowblowers, small snowblowers, and then shovels. Two snowblowers, one large and one small, were assigned to each house, along with two shovels, all of which would handle the driveway, the sidewalks, and any steps.

Mrs. Watson had set up her hot-chocolate and hot-apple-cider station to help keep everyone warm and everyone's energy up as walkways were cleared, while some of the other families brought over cookies and other baked goods. The Nelsons made their clothes dryer available to quickly dry wet gloves so fingers did not get too cold. In no time, every driveway was cleared, and then the snowplow came through and put a lot of the snow back where it had been at the foot of the driveways, because that's what snowplows do!

All the kids had helped, and all the kids had played. Snow forts were built. Snow families were built. A huge snow dragon with wings and a long tail appeared on one lawn. Snow angels were made. Snow ice cream was made, eaten, and enjoyed. Dogs caught snowballs and dug tunnels in almost every yard. Moms stopped snow-covered feet and jackets in the garages before those wearing them could enter into the houses, and dogs were toweled down there too. There was a lot of talking and a lot of laughter. A snow day was a lot of fun.

While one snow day might be a lot of fun, three snow days were beginning to become a little boring. Games had been played. Books had been read. Snow forts, snow angels, snowmen, snow women, snow children, and snow cream had all been made. By this time most of the streets had been cleared, but it was still hard to get from place to place because many parking lots were big blankets of snow. Looking for something for The Family to do, The Mother discovered that the parking lot and most of the walking paths at Fox Hill Park had been cleared.

One of the many nice things about living in Bowie was that there were many open park areas and game fields where kids and families could play and have a good time outside. Fox Hill Park was one of those places, and it was also close to The Wilkinsons' home. Even though the past days had been unusually cold, with a little bundling up, a nice walk around the pond might be fun.

"My Beloved, are you sure that you want to join us this afternoon? It will be freezing cold outside even with your new coat from Emma-Gene. I do not wish for you to be uncomfortable."

The cat rubbed against The Big Dog once again marking him as her own. "My Anthony, I am planning to stay in the van, where it will be much warmer. Even in the van, it will still be nice to be out of the house for a little while. Also it gives me an opportunity to wear Emma-Gene's beautiful new green coat and hat. I won't even have to bother with the boots because I will be in the van. So you can have fun in your way with The Boys, and I can still be with you and have fun in my way, not with The Boys."

The van was still parked in the driveway. The Family garage still contained the new snowblower, generator, extra gas for the grill, cut wood for the fireplace, and cases of bottled water. In the extra steps it took to get into the van, everyone could truly feel the biting cold. To herself, The Mother wondered if this little adventure was really such a good idea.

All of those thoughts disappeared for the moment when The Family arrived at The Pond and looked out at the new land that they were about to explore. Yes, the parking lot had been cleared. Yes, they could see that some of the walking paths had also been cleared, but everything else had the strange smooth and bumpy shape of some foreign white world. Tree branches bent, weighted down with their new white leaves. Bushes, grills, benches, and tables had become strange misshapen bumps underneath their heavy white coats. Everything looked both familiar and completely different. And it was terribly cold. With no houses to block it or tree leaves to slow it down, the wind that cut through was bitter, harsh, and brutal. It was a wind that could take a person's breath away.

Once again, as they were getting out of the van, The Mother thought that maybe this was not such a good idea. She found herself looking at Cleopatra, who had taken over the warm spot The Mother had just left in her seat, and hoping the cat would somehow give her an excuse to call off the walk.

"Michael, maybe we should rethink this. It's much colder out here than I thought it would be. Cleopatra Is going to be in the van by herself, and it's going to get cold in there fast."

"Oh, come on, Honey. It will be fine. Look, Big Tony and The Boys are already off and running in the new snow." He pointed toward the threesome. Yes, the call of snow with no footprints had certainly reached out to Anthony and The Boys. Still unable to get rid of the feeling that this was no longer a good idea, The Mother tried once again.

"But I didn't put Anthony's coat on him, and he has so little fur to keep him warm. I know that you don't want him to catch a cold."

"Michelle, what's with you today, honey? Anthony's got more muscle mass to keep him warm than I do. He's been fine for the past three days in the snow, and he'll be fine now. Sure, it is cold, but we're not going to be here that long. So let's leave the cat in the van, and once we get moving, you'll feel better about everything." As the van door slid closed, The Father took his wife's hand, and they began to follow The Boys and Anthony down one of the paths. As they walked, Michael and Michelle passed a few other people all bundled up, and they all laughed at themselves for having cabin fever and being so silly as to be out in the cold like this.

Meanwhile Anthony and The Boys jumped, ran, and rolled in the snow as if they had never seen or played in snow before and would never have the opportunity to do so again. The Boys and Anthony had gotten away from The Parents by a good bit, and the biting wind made the sounds of their laughter seem even farther away. They were racing to the top of a rather tall hill that took a long sloping drop before crossing one of the unplowed pathways and invisibly blending into the snow-covered ice on the pond below.

Again, The Mother had that queasy feeling. "Michael, tell The Boys to wait for us. I don't like them to be so far away. Even in snow this deep, you can lose your balance and fall. It can still be slip-per-y..."

Suddenly time almost stopped, and both parents stood motionless and helpless. They watched what happened next in the slow motion that only happens when something really terrible occurs right in front of you.

～⟩Π⟨～

Jeffrey was three years older than his little brother, and he would be taller than him for many years to come, but seven-year-old Little Bobby was tough and strong. So when Jeffrey reached the top of the hill first and began to jump up and down in celebration with his climbing partner Big Tony, his little brother was angry and frustrated at being beaten once again by his brother's longer, stronger legs. In his moment of blind anger, the younger boy put his head down and plowed himself full force right into the middle of his brother's chest, because that is what younger brothers sometimes do when they have been beaten once again.

The older boy, caught off guard, had his breath completely knocked out of him. He dropped like a limp wet towel into a heap on the snow. The deep snow did not hold him in place. The Boy's body—padded and weighted by two sweaters, two pairs of pants, two pairs of socks, heavy boots, a baseball cap, a jacket with a hood over the cap, heavy mittens, and a scarf tied around his neck—began to roll down the hill, picking up snow as it went. Jeffrey had become a giant human snowball that picked up more snow and more speed as it rolled down the hill. Down the hill, the snow-boy-ball rolled. He rolled past the unplowed pathway and across the snow-covered line of the land, continuing not only until he reached what had to be the water but until he was over the *deep* part of the pond.

First, there was quiet as the snow-boy-ball finally came to a stop. Then there was the horrible groaning sound of the thin layer of ice under deep snow trying to adjust to the unexpected weight of a snow-boy-ball. Next there was an equally horrible quiet. Finally came the most terrifying sound of all as the weight of the snow-boy-ball became too much for the thin layer of ice. It began to crack and then to break apart, letting the snow-boy-ball sink into the freezing waters beneath it.

Anthony had followed the rolling mass of snow and boy down the hill, trying to grab some part of Jeffrey's jacket to stop him, but The Mastiff's weight and thick tree-trunk legs sank him deep into the snow, slowing him down. Anthony watched as His Boy got farther and farther away from him, until he reached a spot that even The Big Dog knew had to be over the water. He paused for just a moment just as Jeffrey stopped thirty feet in front of him. He also heard the first groan of the ice, followed by the silence and then the horrible breaking. What happened next would seem impossible to humans, but it happened anyway. The two-hundred-pound Mastiff took two or three steps backward and then took a flying leap, sailing into the air, somehow crossing the distance from the land to the hole of snow and ice into which His Boy had disappeared.

The impact of his massive body crashing through the frozen pond sent shards of ice and snow exploding several feet into the air. Once again the following silence was horrible as Michael and Michelle Wilkinson stood holding on to each other, not knowing if they would ever see Their Son or Their Dog again.

"Where's Jeffrey? Where's Tony?" Bobby shrieked as he came running down the hill. "Jeffrey fell down the hill, but where did he go?"

Just then arose the groaning sound of moving water and more breaking ice, as if something were coming up from the bottom of a deep well with high sides all around it. The Parents watched in happy disbelief as they saw Jeffrey's head emerge from the water, resting on top of Anthony's. His limp body was wrapped around His Dog almost as if he were taking a nap on him.

Michael Wilkinson was already reaching into his coat pocket for his cell phone. "I'll 911 one while you take Bobby back to the van. Whatever is to happen here, he doesn't need to see it."

"I'm not leaving Jeffrey." Michelle Wilkinson was trying to control her voice for the sake of her other son.

"Once the fire engines get here, other people will arrive. There will be someone who can stay with Bobby, and you can come back then. Go now." The Father took Bobby's hand, put it into His Wife's, and almost pushed them both away toward the parking lot, while Bobby continued to protect. "Why's Jeffrey sleeping on Anthony in the water? Isn't the water cold? I don't want to go to the van. I want to go in the water with Anthony too."

⌒⋏⋏⋏

Hakeem Price had been a member of the Bowie Fire Department for a long time, and this was the kind of call that he hated the most. "Come on, guys, time to saddle up. A boy and his dog have gone through the ice at Fox Hill Pond. From what the dispatcher said, it's a big dog, and he's holding the boy up out of the water. So we've got two lives to save here: the boy's first, and then if we can, the dog's. So let's move it."

Instead of running for their gear and equipment in the usual mass of men and women, they all stopped where they stood and looked at Hakeem. Most of the people looking at him had worked with The Captain for a long time. Like most coworkers, during their downtime they all talked about their family and friends with each other. They all knew that Michael Wilkinson and The Captain had been friends since they were young kids together. Most of them had met both Michael's boys and Hakeem's girls at the fire station at one time or another. They knew that each set of children called the other man "uncle" because the two men were as close as any brothers. Every time these men and women left the station, they all knew that someone's life could be at risk, so every call, every life, every time was important. And this one could possibly be family to them—very close family.

Hakeem looked back at all the silent eyes gazing at him. He worked beside these people day and night. He knew that they were thinking all the things that he was afraid to think himself. This time he spoke more slowly and sounded less in charge.

"Come on, guys. Give me a break here. I know that there's a good chance that could be one of Mike's boys and his dog Anthony. So this might be my godson, and I guess you could call him my goddog too. If this is Mike and one of his sons, and if the worst should happen, I want to be able to look at my best friend and his wife in the face and tell them, just like we would to anyone else, that you guys did everything humanly possible to save their child. *SO LET'S MOVE IT!*"

⌒⋔⋏⋂

The Mother had left Cleopatra in the perfect spot in the front seat of the van. The sun was coming in at just the right angle to warm her. She was curled up inside her beautiful new emerald-green coat with its matching hat. All was quiet and peaceful, and suddenly she heard a loud groaning sound. The cat's head shot up, but, of course, she could not see anything from where she was on the seat. Then all was quiet. Maybe she had drifted off, and the sound was part of a dream that she could not remember. No, because now there was an even louder and much bigger *breaking* and *crashing* sound!

"ANTHONY!" she screamed. It was Her Anthony. Something had happened to him. Something horrible. The cat reared up on her hind legs, but she could not see anything but snow. She tore at the window, knowing her claws could do nothing to the glass. She leaped into the back seat, hoping against hope that somehow the glass or doors might be different. She clawed at both, but, of course, nothing happened. Helpless and unable to think, she ripped chunks from the front seats with her teeth in the ridiculous hope that she could somehow bite and tear her way through the van. It tasted horrible, but at least something was moving. Then she heard it—the hum of the motor and then the back door beginning to slide open. It was The Mother!

Anyone who has been granted the privilege of living with a cat or anyone who has had the responsibility of rescuing a cat is well aware of the fact that cats have mastered the secret of body liquefaction. The Internet is full of pictures and videos of cats who have gotten themselves into and, in most cases, out of amazingly small, cramped, tight places. So as soon as the van door opened about two inches, Cleopatra quickly liquefied and escaped. She heard just enough of The Mother's voice caught in the wind, calling, "Cleopatra, come back!"

⌒⌒⌒

Michael Wilkinson had been pacing back and forth for what seemed like an hour, at least, but as he looked at his watch again, he knew it had really only been about three minutes since he had called 911. He had tried to be calm and patient as the dispatcher asked question after question—his name, his address, his location.

Did the boy seem to be conscious?

How long had the boy and the dog been in the water?

Was there a clear road that the fire truck could drive through?

He wished that he could just go and grab his son himself. But for years, Hakeem had told him stories of parents doing just that kind of thing. Almost always they ended up making matter worse by some how getting injured themselves. So he had fought back the urge to scream at the man, "Just get them here! This is my son and my dog, so just get the trucks here!"

He told himself he had to be calm in case Jeffrey could hear him; he did not want to frighten The Boy more than he already might be. He told himself that he had to give the dispatchers all the information that they asked for so the firefighters would have the equipment they needed when they arrived and would not have to waste precious time sending for more. Michael Wilkinson could not help himself. He looked at his watch again because he was The Father to both This Boy and This Dog, and more than anything, he wanted to take both of them back home safely.

The Father heard a voice calling and looked toward the parking lot to see his wife standing near their van. Rushing away from her and toward him was a small streak of green leaping across the snow. Cleopatra's weight and speed kept her from falling into the snow. Her feet hardly touched the cold wet flakes as she rushed to Her Anthony. She did not realize that she was on snow on top of ice until she reached the deep hole in the three feet of snow and had to look down to see Her Beloved below in the icy water with The Boy, Jeffrey, on his back. The Boy still lay on his stomach with his head resting on The Big Dog's head and with his feet and hands dangling limp in the ten feet of frigid water below him.

The Mastiff sensed that His Lady was near and tried to look up at her, but he could not see anything but the wall of snow in front of him.

"Do not worry, My Anthony," Cleopatra called to him. "I will come to you."

"N-n-no, My Lovely, The...the...Fa-fa-father will see you." The Big Dog was treading water to keep himself afloat and as much of His Boy as possible out of the water. "I can do this. I can ke-keep The Boy's head out of the water. If he still lives, I will not let him drown no matter what that means for me. The Father has already called for help, and they will be here soon."

Cleopatra ignored Anthony completely; her only response was to call out, "Loving and Almighty Bastet, please give me the strength to do what must be done. Give My Beloved, The Noble Anthony, the strength to save The Boy he loves, and give The Humans the means to save them both."

Suddenly the air filled with a flash of blinding bright-green light. Michael Wilkinson, who had been standing on the other side of the pond, had seen his cat in her emerald-green coat come running toward the huge hole in the ice. He watched Cleopatra as she sat on the edge for a moment, looking at Anthony and His Son down in the water. Then the flash of green light blinded him. He had to step back and raise his arms to shield his eyes, as the light was so strong and bright. Then, as quickly as it had come, the light was gone. When he looked again, all the snow around Cleopatra seemed to have melted, leaving her an open path extending close to twenty feet long and six feet wide, almost as if a snowplow had come through and brought her down to the same level as Anthony.

Now Cleopatra looked directly into Anthony's blue-brown eyes and said to him, "My Beloved, look at me, only me. There is no cold water; there is only me. There is no extra weight on your back—no boy and no heavy wet clothes. It is only you and I. Soon you will hear the noise and the voices of the humans who will come to help you and Your Boy, but you will only see and listen to me. Bastet and I will keep you warm and keep you safe. This I promise you, My Beloved."

⌒⋏⟆

Feeling completely helpless, The Mother stood by the van and watched her cat race across the ice toward The Dog and His Boy. There was nothing she could do right now to help either of them. She needed to get Bobby inside the van and out of the cold. As she got him into the back and helped him into his booster seat, she realized there was someone else sitting in the front seat. She turned, ready to scream in a new kind of fear, and then she realized who it was.

"Good Grief, Auntie Emma-Gene! What in the world are you doing here?" The usual questions quickly followed: "Where did you come from, and how did you get into the van?"

"Oh, none of those things matter, my dear. I'm here because right now you need me. I came to take Bobby home so you can stay with Michael and Jeffrey."

The Mother sighed with relief. She wanted to ask twenty different questions, but instead she just turned to the other woman and said, "Thank you, Auntie."

"Well, of course, Sweetie," said the curly-haired woman. "Now, go on back down the hill, and I'll take care of everything."

Michelle began to back out through the door, but then she remembered that her house was locked. She quickly ducked back inside to say, "Here is the key," or "How are you going to get in?" or something like that, only to find that she was in the van by herself. Both Auntie and Bobby were gone!

The Mother again found herself ready to scream, but before she could, a blinding green light seemed to engulf the car and everything around her. She raised her arms to protect her eyes from the light, but almost as soon as it had appeared, it was gone. For a moment Michelle Wilkinson got into her van, sat down, and looked around her. This was all just so ridiculous and, at the same time, so very horrible. Somehow her youngest son had just disappeared with a strange little lady whom everyone called "Auntie" even though no one had any idea whom she might be related to. Her older son was lying unconscious—at least she prayed that he was just unconscious— on the back of the family dog in freezing water in the middle of a pond, and yet, she felt that at the end of this day, everything was going to be all right. She did not know how, but somehow everyone she loved was going to be safe.

Hearing the sound of approaching sirens, she jumped out of the van. She laughed at herself as she closed and locked the van as if that would keep Auntie Emma-Gene out. Then she ran down the hill to be with her husband, son, dog, and cat.

⌒⁊⋔⋋

The Father also heard the sound of the approaching rescuers. Finally the first engine came into sight, followed by another and another in what seemed to be an endless parade. He wasn't sure why, but for a brief moment, The Father found himself hoping no one else in the city, or maybe even the county, had any type of emergency because he was pretty certain that every piece of emergency equipment available was there for His Son and His Dog.

The Fire Commanders' SUV arrived, and the door swung open. Out stepped Hakeem Price in full white command gear. Whatever your rank might be, from Sargent to Captain, when you were the one in charge of the call, you became The Commander. The Father ran over to his friend and hugged him, saying, "I was hoping it would be you who came."

Hakeem hugged his lifelong friend back and said, "I was hoping it wouldn't be you, with my godson and my goddog." For a brief second, the two men smiled at each other. Then Hakeem asked, "Which one is it?"

"Jeffrey." It was all The Father could bring himself to say. Then Hakeem looked over and saw Michelle, out of breath from running, joining them. He gave her a hug, winked at her, and said, "Don't worry; I haven't lost a boy or a dog yet today, and I don't plan to start with one of my own!"

Turning from best friend into Commander, he looked from the hole in the ice back up the hill and said, "OK, I can see where the two boys started at the top of the hill, and it looks like there might have been some celebration at the top. Jeffrey got there first, didn't he?"

Not waiting for an answer, he continued, "Bobby probably got mad because Jeffrey beat him once again and took his brother out." Hakeem had watched The Boys grow and play all their lives, so he was well aware of how each would have reacted.

He continued, "Now, I can see the path Jeffrey took rolling down, but what in the world happened about halfway down? Where did that section come from that looks to be about twenty or thirty feet long and six feet wide? It looks like it was somehow plowed, and it goes right up to where the dog and the cat are. I can tell from where the benches are that it has to be well into the water. I can see how the boy could have rolled that far out into the pond, but for the life of me, I don't see how a dog Anthony's size and weight could have leaped as far as he did to get to the boy and just make one hole. Anyway, somehow he did, and that's the important part. He's a big dog. He should be able to hold the boy for a while, but that water is freezing cold, and it's already been about six or eight minutes. We don't want to push our luck here. We've got to get them out of there as fast as we can. The boy first and then the dog."

Like everyone in Bowie, Hakeem had heard the stories about Cleopatra and the strange things that sometimes happened when she was around. He looked at her in her green coat as she sat on the ice and snow and gazed at Anthony. He turned back to Michael and Michelle and said, "Some other time I'll ask you how all that snow melted and got your cat down to the same level as the dog, but we don't have time for that now."

The Father shook his head. "I have no idea. I just remember this dazzling green light that I had to shield my eyes from. And when I could see again, there was the path, and Cleopatra was there with Anthony."

Hakeem said, "Yes, we saw the green light too as we were coming up the road."

And The Mother added, "I saw it too as I left Bobby with Auntie Emma-Gene."

To which both men responded in unison, "Auntie Emma-Gene is here? How did she—"

The Mother quickly interrupted them. "OK, focus, guys! Boy and dog in the freezing water! I'll fill you in on Auntie later."

All three adults went quiet. They looked from each other to Cleopatra and back again and then promised to talk about it later.

The Commander turned to his crew and yelled out, "Come on, guys. Get out the kits with the drills so we can test the ice to see what kind of thickness we have here. You guys over there, start pulling out those ladders. We've got some lives to save here."

Then he turned to Michael and Michelle in best-friend mode again. "For the next couple of minutes—and I promise you it will be just a couple of minutes—it's going to look like we're not doing a whole lot, but we are. We are going to do a quick test to see how thick the ice is so we can tell how much weight it can support. We don't want to waste any time rescuing the rescuers. So we have to have a plan, and we have to do it right the first time. I want my godson out of there, and I want to see that monster Mastiff of yours playing with my two Danes again. So hang tight, and I'll be right back."

Until their friend had left them, Michael and Michelle had not realized just how many men and women were there. Four EMTs (Emergency

Medical Technicians) had come closer, carrying a basket-like stretcher between them. They also carried extra blankets and two large cases of medical equipment. A few more had worked their way over to the edge of the water and were using a hand drill to pull out plugs of ice so that they could measure the thickness. The Wilkinsons saw two men who had removed their outer boots, pants, and jackets to reveal heavy-duty cold-water wet suits in case they had to go into the freezing water. Someone had brought a pretty-good-sized inflatable boat. Still others were laying down ladders like railroad tracks on the new strangely snowplowed area that lead directly to The Boy, The Dog, and The Cat. Michael Wilkinson put what he hoped was a reassuring arm around his wife's shoulders. "It won't be long now. They'll have them both out soon."

～⁊⫯⫯⫯～

With the parking lot cleared, Dr. Daisy had finally been able to get back into her office. Before the big snowstorm, all her patients had been either sent home or moved to larger Animal Hospitals that had twenty-four-hour staff, but there was still one pet to be taken care of. Most veterinary offices have house pets that live there all the time. Such pets can be any kind of animal depending on the kind of practice the vet has. Vets like Dr. Daisy who specialize in small animals and house pets usually have a dog, cat, bird, or maybe a hamster. During stressful times these in-house animals can be comforting to both the pet and the human parent.

Dr. D had taken her two parrots home with her in their cage before the storm. Her little shaggy black mixed-breed dog, Sunny Boy, whom she brought to the office almost daily, had of course gone home with her as usual, but because cats do not take well to changes in their environment, she had left the cat, The Mighty Trity, at the office. As long as cats have an adequate food supply, clean water, and a clean litter box, they can be left alone for a couple of days and be very content. After that they tend to get a little lonely. So it was a very happy big three-legged orange purring boy who met her when she got back into the office.

When The Mighty Trity was a kitten, Dr. Daisy had found him with a horrible infection in his right front leg. It was so bad that the doctor had to amputate it in order to save his life. The little kitten had been so sweet and affectionate that Dr. Daisy and her Vet Tech, Suzanne, had decided to keep him. Now, when he felt like it, he greeted the arrivals at the office and donated blood to other cats that might need it during surgery. The big orange ball of purring fur was on the desk with her as the vet tried to check her messages and do some paperwork, which was slowed down considerably by the big cat's assistance as he tried to chase her cursor around her computer screen with his one front arm. It was almost a relief when the phone rang and released her from the battle with the cat, which she was losing. The caller ID said "Bowie Animal Shelter." The doctor sighed as she reached for the phone. It was not unusual for animals to get hurt during bad weather.

"Hi, this is Dr. Daisy."

"Oh, Dr. D, I'm so glad that you're in your office today." It was Jennifer from the shelter, and she sounded excited and worried. "I just heard something over the police scanner, and I don't know why, and I'm not sure, but I had to try to reach you because I think that it's one of yours."

Many animal shelters had police scanners so that they could hear the police officers talking. Many times it was the police who found a lost or injured animal, and the scanner let the shelter staff know if they needed to go and help. This time, though, Jennifer was rambling on so much that Dr. D could not understand what the other woman was talking about.

"Jennifer, dear, you're going to have to slow down a bit because I have no idea what or who you're talking about."

"OK, Dr. D. I'm sorry. I'll try to get it together." The young woman took a deep breath before she continued, "A notice came over the police scanner saying that there had been an accident at Fox Hill Pond. A boy had fallen through the ice, and a big dog had gone into the water after him. The dog was holding the boy out of the water on his back." She paused for a moment and took another deep breath before going on. "Dr. D, I don't know why, but for some reason I feel almost certain that it's one of the boys that I sent to you from the family that had adopted that Big Mastiff and that strange cat with all the jewelry. If the fire department can get them all out alive, I'm sure that they will bring the dog to you."

"Jennifer, I understand your concern, but I can't do anything until someone calls me, and I haven't heard anything yet." The words had barely left her lips when the other phone line began to ring. This time the caller ID said "M Wilkinson." Quickly the doctor said, "I've got to go. There's a call coming in on the other line, and this may be it. I'll keep you posted."

⌒⍒⌐

"Anthony. *Anthony!* ANTHONY, *LOOK AT ME!*"

"I am s-s-sorry, My Lovely. It is not you. It is the c-c-cold. You being h-h-here gives me g-g-great strength and c-c-comfort."

"The Mother and The Father have called the Fire Department. It appears that the same people who put out fires also do cold-water rescue. The noise you heard came from the trucks with all the equipment. Humans never know how to do anything quietly. The person in charge seems to be The Boys' Uncle Hakeem. You know, Sebastian and Julia's Humans. They have been talking a lot, as humans always do, and they have pulled out a lot of equipment all over the place, including a small boat, for some reason. I think that they may almost be ready to finally do something." Cleopatra could not control the frustration in her voice. The retrieval of Her Anthony, and, of course, The Boy too, seemed to be moving so slowly.

"It's all right, My L-l-lovely. How is The Boy?"

"His skin is pale, and his lips seem to be rather blue. I do not think that is usual in humans, is it? I think that I hear just a little of his breathing."

Cleopatra had lost the matching hat to her coat as she ran across the snow to Anthony, so her thin cat ears were exposed and very cold. She wished that she had bothered to wear the matching boots that Auntie Emma-Gene had made for her, because her paws were freezing as she sat on the ice, but she kept these things to herself. Whatever cold she was feeling, she knew that Her Anthony was feeling a thousand times more.

"Yes, My B-b-boy still lives. It is slow, but I can still feel his heartbeat even through all his clothes. Just like at h-h-home when he is lying on me. My Boy lives." Even Anthony could feel that his words were coming more slowly, with longer pauses between them. In order to stay afloat, he had to keep his legs moving, but he was so cold. Though Scout and Reagan, the Newfoundlands, have complained about their thick heavy coats on the hot, humid summer days, right now he wished that he had the water dogs' triple-thick and almost waterproof coats. He just had to keep his legs moving. It would not be long now. Soon His Boy would be safe, and he could stop. He could rest.

"ANTHONY! MY ANTHONY! LOOK AT ME!" This time there was no hiding the panic in Cleopatra's voice. There was also no hiding that the cold was beginning to have its effect on the Big Mastiff.

"I am sorry, My Lady. I will be all right. I am just so tired and so very cold." Cleopatra could hear the fatigue and shivering, life-draining cold in Her Beloved's voice and wondered how much longer he could keep this up.

"ANTHONY, I WILL BE RIGHT BACK!" The Cat in the green coat began to run across the snow-covered ice, dodging firefighters and equipment and single-mindedly heading in one direction, toward The Mother.

〰

Hakeem returned to his friends. "We've had a couple of little things to slow us down, but we're pretty much ready to go. The problem has been that we have two different kinds of ice here. We have clear ice from the pond itself and what's called white ice from the snow. The clear ice is the strongest, but we only have maybe two inches of it at best, and that's not enough to support anything. We have more of the white ice, but it's not as strong. You usually need two inches of white ice to every inch of clear. So in a perfect world, we would need at least four to maybe five inches of clear ice to be perfectly safe, and that would mean we would need eight to ten inches of snow ice. As you know, we do not live in a perfect world, so this is what we've got to work with: we've got just shy of two inches of clear and about three and a half of snow, which should give the equivalent of about three and a half inches of good solid ice, when we would really like to see at least four."

"Hakeem, what does that mean?" The Mother could no longer control the impatience that was growing in her voice.

He put his hand on her shoulder to try to reassure her. He looked at her and his best friend and said, "It means that we're going to play the hand that we were dealt and work with what we've got. We've laid out the two rows of ladders going straight up to them. These two guys right here in the wet suits and safety cords are going to crawl up the ladders on their bellies to spread out their weight. They will be pulling the inflatable along with them, which also has a rope on it with guys on the other end. If nothing goes wrong, when these two get up to Jeffrey, they will grab him off of Anthony and put him into the boat. The guys on the other end of the rope will pull him back as fast as humanly possible. The EMTs are waiting to get him, and you will all head off to the hospital. On the other hand, if the ice should begin to give way, the wet suit guys are prepared to go into the water, get the boy, and put him and themselves into the boat. They will all get pulled back in together, and off to the hospital you go."

The Father opened his mouth as if he was going to say something, and then he stopped. Reading his friend's mind, Hakeem continued, "Don't worry, Mike. Once you and Michelle are on your way with The Boy, we'll be going after Anthony."

The Mother broke in. "Michael has already called Dr. Daisy, so take Anthony there. She'll be waiting for him."

Their friend nodded and said, "That's good to know. Now this part is hard. I know that you'd like to take Jeffrey to the Health Center because it's so close, but I've called ahead to the larger hospital in Annapolis." He looked at Michelle and could see the fear rising in her eyes again. "Anthony's been able to keep Jeffrey's body, his core, pretty much up and out of the cold water, but his feet and hands have been in for a while now. If there is a problem with the cold water affecting his fingers, hands, toes, or feet, the larger hospital will be better able to handle it. In fact the specialist is already on his way in." Trying to reassure them both, he went on, "It may not be a problem at all. I just wanted to be prepared just in case. I kissed all those toes and fingers when he was a baby, and I don't want to lose any of them.

"One last thing. I know that one of you will want to be in the ambulance with him, but with the EMTs and what they have to do, there just isn't going to be any room. What you're going to have to do is follow them in your car. There will be a police car behind you, so, Mike, please try to keep up." As men do, Hakeem gave his friend a soft punch on the arm to try to get him to smile. It kind of worked.

"So!" The Commander was back. "You two will have the boy; I will have the dog...and the cat, and we'll keep in touch by phone." Then he turned to the waiting firefighters. "OK, now is the time, you guys. Let's do it. Do it fast, and do it safe. We don't have time to rescue any of you."

⌒〵〴⌒

Michael and Michelle Wilkinson had been standing at the line between land and water, looking for signs of life in their son and, at the same time, trying to stay out of the way of the people who were there to help. Part of Fox Hill Park faced and could be seen from a major roadway. All the flashing lights and multicolored pieces of equipment had attracted quite a crowd from passing traffic. Word spread quickly that a child and his dog had gone through the ice. The people who had come were not just onlookers; many had brought coffee for the firefighters. Others offered hot chocolate to The Parents. One older lady insisted Michelle take a handmade quilt from her, saying The Mother would need something to wrap Her Boy in when she took him home. Even chairs were offered. At a time when they were both feeling so completely helpless, they also both felt completely loved and taken care of.

As The Mother's eyes panned the crowd around them—firefighters, EMTs, friends, neighbors, and strangers—her eyes once again went to the hole in the ice, where Anthony and Jeffrey were, with Cleopatra in her green coat sitting beside them, except Cleopatra was no longer there. Trying to remain calm, Michelle turned to her husband. "Michael, where is Cleopatra?"

"Well, she's..." Michael stopped because not only was she not with Anthony and The Boy, but now he could also see a spot of bright green racing across the ice, jumping over equipment, dodging around people, and heading right toward them. "Well, she's right here."

The Cat took one flying leap that spanned four feet and dove right into the middle of The Mother's chest. The unexpected impact made Michelle step back and drop the hot chocolate she had been holding, as she reached out to support and hold The Cat. Michael Wilkinson saw his wife reach out to grab Cleopatra. At the same time, once The Cat was still, he saw her put two paws, which had to be ice cold, on each side of Michelle's face. For a second he was sure he saw a brief flash of green light moving between the two pairs of eyes, cat and human. Then The Cat jumped down and ran across the ice back toward Anthony and The Boy.

"What in the world was that all about?" He turned to his wife, ready to laugh, until he saw the look of panic and fear on her face. Michelle Wilkinson grabbed her husband's arm, holding him so tight that her hand hurt him even through several heavy layers of clothing.

"Michael, get Hakeem. Get him now. They have to start now. The cold is getting to Anthony, and he can't hold on much longer." The panic rose in her voice. "Michael, we have to get them right now, or we will lose them both!"

The Father had never seen a look like that on his wife's face before or heard the near scream in her voice. Without saying a word, he turned and started running toward his friend, but before he had taken more than a few steps, he saw two men in black wet suits lie down on the ladders and begin to pull themselves across the steps with one hand while the other pulled the inflatable boat that was between them. They moved across the ice toward Anthony, Jeffrey, and the returned Cleopatra. Michael went back to his wife and put his arm around her again. "It's already started, Michelle. It won't be long now."

The two of them and what seemed to be half of the city watched in silence as the two black figures moved slowly along the ladders.

Since they and the ladders were just borderline of the weight the ice would hold, they had to stay flat. That way they could spread out their weight on the surface of the ice and put as little pressure on it as possible. They moved slowly, listening for any sounds that might mean that the ice was going to give way. Finally they reached The Dog with The Boy on his back.

Mark Stevenson, the leader of the two wet suited figures, was a father and a dog owner and lover himself. Almost everyone in the city knew this Big Dog and His Cat companion, who had been sitting nearby on the ice, watching and waiting. So Mark spoke to Anthony.

"Hey, Big Tony, I see that you've been working hard to take good care of Your Boy. Well, my friend and I are going to help you out. We're going to reach out and take Jeffrey off your back. Then we're going to put him in this boat-looking thing that we've been pulling along with us, and some other friends of ours will pull him to safety. Once that is done, we're going to get you out of here because we know that you've got to be cold and tired."

Then, remembering how his own dogs smiled when he said this to them, he added, "You've done a great job, Big Tony. You've been a good boy."

No sooner were the words finished than both men reached out at the same time while still lying on their stomachs; one pushed a hand between Jeffrey's chest and Anthony's back while using the other hand to get a good hold on the back of The Boy's jacket. Jeffrey's legs were hanging down into the water, and the other man grabbed hold of both The Boy's pant legs so that he could pull them together as one.

Getting a tight grip on the child, the two men looked at each other and counted aloud, "One, Two, THREE!"

On "THREE!" they lifted the heavy water-soaked boy up over their heads while twisting their bodies so that they could slide him over the rounded side of the rubber boat. The crowd cheered, but the two men knew that their job was far from over. They walked back down their ladders, still on their stomachs, and pulled some rope, some hatchets, and something that looked like a big leather band out of the boat before signaling the men on the land who held the rope tied to the boat. The four firefighters on the rope pulled with all their strength to get The Boy and the boat to them as fast as possible.

As soon as the two firefighters in the black wet suits got to Jeffrey, Michael and Michelle Wilkinson had begun running to their car. As the boat and The Boy were pulled onto land, two of the EMTs lifted him out of the boat and into one of the basket-like stretchers. Then four men, one at each corner, ran The Boy toward the waiting ambulance. Once they were inside, everyone waited in silence until a head popped out of the open door and a voice yelled out, "We've got a heartbeat!"

There was an audible sigh of relief from the crowd, followed by an absolute roar of cheering as the doors closed and the big truck's red and yellow light lit up. Its sirens came to life, and it began to move slowly at first onto the road toward the parking lot. The Wilkinsons pulled their van in behind it, and The Bowie Police Car moved behind them, with its red and blue light on and its sirens going. Once again the crowd cheered as the three vehicles took off on their way to the larger hospital in Annapolis.

⌒⋙⌐

As the whine of the sirens faded away, Mark Stevenson and his partner, Jim Green, turned again to Anthony. "OK, Big Fella, you've taken care of Your Boy, and now it's your turn." Mark and Jim had taken part in a lot of animal rescues, and they knew that half of the job was trying to keep the animals calm so that they did not hurt themselves any more than they might already be and so that they did not hurt the rescuers out of fear. They had both met Anthony several times at the firehouse with Mike and Hakeem, so they felt that they knew The Big Mastiff well enough to try something a little different.

"Now, you're a really Big Boy, Anthony, so I don't think that we can lift you out like we did Your Boy. We know that you have to be pretty cold and tired by now, but we're going to need your help so that we can get you back home to Your Boy. Now, my partner, Jim, is going to slide into this cold water with you. He's going to have a big nylon harness with him that's going to be attached to a rope. Jim is going to try to get the band underneath you and then tie the two sides together with the rope. That's so we'll have a good grip on you and won't lose you, but you'll have to be as still as you can and help Jim."

Mark had never taken the time before to explain to an animal what they were doing, but he had heard the stories, some of which he did not believe, about this particular dog and cat. He thought that it might be worth a try to talk to him. Many animals fought against the very people who were trying to help them. If the Big Guy could somehow understand, if he could work with them and not fight against them out of fear, it would make their job a lot easier, and they'd be able to get him out of the freezing water a lot faster.

Jim slipped into the water with one end of the heavy rope while his friend and partner, Mark, held the other end. They let the wide band of the harness rest on Anthony's back for a moment so that he would know what it was and what it felt like. Then the two men slowly moved the band over The Big Dog's back and down over his tail. It was Jim's job to get the band under the dog's back legs and against his chest so that they could grab both sides around him. For this to work, the dog had to stay relatively still instead of kicking or thrashing around in the water. Mark tried to talk in a soothing and calming voice, but Anthony only looked at the cat sitting on the ice in front of him.

Her unprotected feet were freezing, but Cleopatra would not move. After she left The Mother, she had returned once again to be by Her Beloved Anthony's side. It was hard for him to talk to her now, so she talked to him. She told him everything about how the men had gotten Jeffrey, even though he had been able to feel the relief of His Boy's weight being taken off him. He had only been able to smile a rather lopsided smile at her. Now it was his turn.

"Not much longer, My Beloved. Your Boy is on his way to the human doctors, and when I was with The Mother, I saw in her eyes that Her Husband had talked to Dr. Daisy, telling her to expect us. It is almost over, My Love."

The plan had been that, if the ice would hold his weight, Mark would hold the ropes and the harness together and pull from his side while Jim, in the water, would try to lift and push Anthony onto the ice. Then Jim would get back onto his ladder, and the two men together would pull The Big Dog over the ice to a waiting blanket and Hakeem's big SUV. It was a good plan. It just did not work.

They pulled, lifted, and pushed Anthony, but as soon as his body covered a few inches of the ice, the ledge would break off and plunge him back into the water. But the two men kept trying. Then one of the sharp pieces of ice cut through the harness and into the dog's side. Once they saw blood in the water and on the ice, they knew that they had to stop. Their own weight, with that of the ladders and then the dog, was just too much for the ice. The only way now was to use the hatchets to cut a path through the ice to pull and guide Anthony through. It would take a lot of time and work, and they could already tell that the cold was taking its toll on The Big Dog.

For the first time ever, Cleopatra felt that she had lied to Her Beloved. She had trusted The Humans, and they had let her down. She understood that The Humans would save their child first. That is the way of the world; the safety and survival of the young always comes first. Throughout all the centuries, parents, and even nonparents, human and animal alike, have sacrificed themselves to save and ensure the continuation of their species and their bloodline. That is what she and Anthony had done that horrible night for two human children, and today there had been no doubt in her mind that The Boy should be saved first.

Now The Boy with His Parents were on their way to the doctors, and Her Anthony was still in the freezing water. And each and every moment was draining the life out of him. She had made the path for them. Why did they take so long? Why were they so slow and so stupid? Why were they willing to let Her Anthony linger in such pain? She had trusted them. She had promised him that The Humans would save him, but they would not. At least not in time. If The Noble Anthony was to continue to walk beside her, SHE would have to find the way for it to happen herself, and she would have to do it NOW!

⌒⋀⋙

Mark Stevenson reluctantly began to reach for his hatchet, which was lying on the ice. Then his friend of many years said to him, "Mark, hold on for a minute. I may be losing my mind, but I think the ice is melting."

"What in the world are you talking about? It's about twenty-five degrees out here at best. There is no melting happening." Mark fired back, annoyed that his friend could even think of such a ridiculous thing.

"Mark, I'm the one in the water, and I'm sure that I can feel it. The water is feeling warmer to me. Look, look. That jagged edge there. The one that had the blood on it. The blood is gone. The edge is smooth now, and there is a space of about six inches that wasn't there before. I'm not kidding, Mark. Somehow the ice is melting."

This time Mark could see it himself. In the space between the two ladders, where the boat had been, the ice was melting, creating a path for them to pull the dog through. The two men looked at each other, and then they looked at the cat in the green coat, who was walking along on the ice beside them, staring rather intently at the ice as she moved. Later on Mark and Jim would ask each other a lot of questions, but right now Mark realized that he had to move back along his ladder as the ice path kept melting.

Jim shouted to him, "I don't know what in the world is going on," and he paused for a quick moment to take another look at Cleopatra. She was still walking along the ice beside them, and now he could see the bright-green glow in her eyes as she stared at the ice. Since he did not dare say what he was seeing, he just said, "But I do know that the ice is melting a lot faster than we could have hacked away at it. Also the warm water feels pretty good right now."

Mark looked over his shoulder, and he could see the men on the shore spreading out the handled tarp for them to put Anthony on. It would not be long now. In fact the ice seemed to be melting almost faster than he was moving down the ladder.

Finally Jim shouted, "My feet just touched the ground. We're almost there!"

Now everything seemed to move rapidly. The crowd was beginning to cheer again as Mark and Jim got close enough for the other firefighters to help them. Anthony seemed to be almost unconscious, but with lots of hands to help and the rope around him, they were able to pull him onto the tarp. Hakeem's big SUV had already been backed up as close as possible.

With plenty of strong backs and arms to lift and pull, The Noble Anthony was gently lifted into the back of the truck. Once he was in and before anyone could close the back door, Cleopatra jumped into the back with him. One of the newer firefighters reached over to try to get her out, but Hakeem managed to grab the man's arm just in time.

"I wouldn't do that if I were you. These two are good friends, and I'm pretty sure that he'll do better if she's with him." The young man backed away, and The Commander called out to the others, "OK, good work to all of you today. You know what you have to do to pack up. I'll be talking to the hospital and to the vet, so I'll keep you all posted. Once again, good work. Let's pray that by the end of this day, we're still two for two."

⌒⌒⌒

Once Dr. Daisy hung up the phone after talking with Michael Wilkinson, for a moment she sat thinking of everything that she needed to do. It did not take her long to realize that there was no way that she would be able to handle the two-hundred-pound Mastiff by herself. She might get some help from whoever brought him, but she knew that they would not be able to stay long. Like it or not, she was going to have to ask Suzanne to come and help her out, if only for a little while. There was only one problem. When Anthony arrived, it was a pretty sure bet that The Cat, Cleopatra, would be with him, and that had not gone very well for Suzanne in the past. Still, Dr. Daisy knew that she had to try.

"Suzanne, it's Dr. D and I was really hoping that you would be home."

"Hi, Dr. D. What's going on?"

"Well, I finally made it into the office today to take care of The Mighty Trity and, of course, check the e-mail and do some paperwork. About five minutes ago, Jennifer from The Bowie Animal Shelter called. She said that she'd heard over their police scanner that a boy had fallen into the ice at Fox Hill Pond and that his BIG DOG was holding him up."

First there was silence, followed by a very slow inquiry. "You don't think that it's that Mastiff with that cat, do you?"

"Unfortunately," the doctor paused here because she really did not want to say the rest. "I was still on the line with Jennifer, when Michael Wilkinson called in. So honey, I'm sorry, but it is *The Mastiff and The Cat*."

More silence.

Dr. Daisy decided to use this time to move on. "First of all, Cleopatra may not even be with him, but what it comes down to, Suzanne, is that I can't handle the Mastiff by myself. He's just too big and heavy. I'm sure I could get some help from whoever brings him, but they won't be able to stay for long. I'm only going to need you for the first couple of hours or so. After that you can go back home, and I'll spend the night with him."

"OK, I'll be there in about ten minutes or so." It was far from the most enthusiastic response she had ever heard, but at that point Dr. D would take what she could get.

"Suzanne, you're not only a good vet tech but also a good friend. Oh, I almost forgot. I picked up one of those thermometers that are used on humans to take their temperature in their ear. This might be a good time to give it a try."

"Sure." The other woman laughed. "My hair is already white. What else could happen?"

Dr. Daisy had to bite her tongue to keep from saying "Don't ask." Instead she said, "See you when you get here."

Thanks to the magic of cell phones, the EMTs in the ambulance with Jeffrey had been able to talk to The Parents as they raced to the hospital in Annapolis. While The Father drove and concentrated on keeping up with the ambulance, The Mother talked with an EMT named Marcie.

"Mrs. Wilkinson, I know that you'd rather be in here with us, but let me tell you what's going on. First, let me tell you that your boy has a good strong heartbeat. It's slow, but that's very common in these cases. The important part is that it's good and strong. Second, I'll apologize now for having to cut him out of some of his clothing. We had to get him out of it fast, and some things were frozen together."

"That's OK, Marcie. Do whatever you have to do. We can always buy a new jacket or pants. Is he still unconscious?" The Mother was trying hard to sound calm and in control, not like a crazy woman who was afraid her son would die before he got to the hospital.

"Yes, ma'am, but that is probably a good thing because he doesn't need to remember any of this. So we've gotten his clothes off him, and we've wrapped him in blankets. We don't have the warm heated ones like they will at the hospital, but it is a start to warming him up. One thing that I want to prepare you for before we get there is that he's very pale and his lips are rather blue." Marcie heard Michelle Wilkinson gasp at that last part.

"Ma'am, I'm not trying to frighten you; I'm just trying to prepare you. This is just the way that the body works. It's trying to keep the important stuff warm and safe as much as it can, so it's taking the blood away from the outer parts like the skin and lips to make sure the important things like the heart and lungs stay warm and working."

"I understand." The Mother's voice sounded a little stronger. "So what about his feet, fingers, toes, and hands?"

"I'm not a doctor, Mrs. Wilkinson, so I can't say for sure, but so far they're only blue, not the black of possible frostbite that we'd have to worry about. We're almost there, so I'm going to go now, but he's a good strong boy."

The Mother reached out and touched her husband's leg as he drove. "I know," she said. "He takes after his Father. Thanks a lot, Marcie, for taking care of Our Boy this far."

When the caravan of ambulance, van, and police car pulled up in front of the Emergency Room's Entrance, both parents were surprised to see what they guessed to be a group of doctors and nurses standing right inside the door waiting for them. As soon as the ambulance doors opened, they all came pouring out into the cold. Jeffrey was immediately transferred to a wheeled gurney and rushed inside, with Michelle Wilkinson following right behind him, while her husband thanked the EMTs and their police escort and parked the van. The Boy was rushed into a special room that had been set up for his arrival.

The Mother was about to go into the room with him when one of the doctors stopped her.

"Mrs. Wilkinson, I'm Dr. Brady. I know that you want to run right in there and be with your son, but I'm going to ask you to do something that I know will be very hard. We have a lot to do in a very short period of time, so right now I'm going to ask you, and your husband when he gets here, to go in there, tell your son how much you love him, and then let us do what we have to do. What I'm asking is for the two of you to wait here, and as soon as we have him set up, we'll call you in."

The Mother was about to protest, but then she felt her husband's arm around her shoulder and heard him say, "We'll go in together, and then we'll wait right here."

Even though Marcie, the EMT, had warned them, it was still hard for both parents to see their son looking so very pale, wrapped up almost as if he were in some kind of cocoon. The Mother bent over her little boy, kissed him on his so very cold cheek, and whispered tenderly to him, "Mommy and Daddy love you very much, Jeffrey, and we will be right here with you when you wake up."

The Father also kissed his son and whispered to him, "I love you, son. You, me, and Anthony, and your Uncle Hakeem and the Danes, still have a lot of playing to do." Then The Parents let their son in the care of Dr. Brady and his staff and sat and waited.

When Hakeem and one of the firefighters arrived at Dr. Daisy's office, she and Suzanne were all set up and waiting for them. They put all the blankets they could spare over The Big Mastiff as he lay on his six-handled tarp. Even with four of them, it still took a lot of effort to move Anthony, and it would have been even harder with only two. Cleopatra had curled up on his side during the ride, and she stayed there while they moved him inside. It was Dr. Daisy who had to give her the bad news that she would have to move.

"Cleopatra, I'm going to have to ask you to move right now so that we can take care of Your Anthony." Remembering their first meeting, she said,

"We may have to do some things that you might find undignified, but I promise you that we will do only what we have to and that we will do it in the most respectful way. If you would like, I'll take your coat off you. It's wet now, so I don't think that it's keeping you very warm anymore. After that you can sit right here." The doctor patted the stainless steel exam table next to where Anthony lay on the floor. "Here you can watch everything if you want to, and when we're finished, you can join him again."

The cat immediately jumped onto the metal surface of the table and sat quietly while her rather soggy coat was removed. Then she crouched down so that she could watch what was happening below.

"First, I have to take his temperature so we'll know just how good or bad things are." The temperature taking went on without incident, but the news was not good. The Big Dog's temperature was only 96 degrees, when it should have been somewhere between 99 and 102.

She turned to Hakeem and the other firefighter and said, "We're going to have to work fast." She reached for a stack of towels that was on the counter behind her. "Commander, if you and your friend will give us a hand here for just a few minutes, I would really appreciate it." She tossed the men some of the towels. Suzanne already had a stack of her own. The doctor continued, "We have to dry him off the best that we can before we move him to the mattress and warming blankets we have set up over there. We have to be somewhat gentle when we rub him with the towels. His skin is a bit tougher than ours, but we still don't want to cause any cell damage from the cold if we can help it."

They all knelt down beside Anthony and gently began to dry him.

Then Hakeem said, "Doctor, I need to let you know that he has a cut from the ice on his other side. It hasn't bled much because of the cold, but it could start once he begins to get warm."

"Thanks for letting me know. I'll take a look when we roll him over. I may have to put a couple of stitches in it."

Without even realizing it, all of them except the young firefighter turned their eyes to Cleopatra, waiting for her reaction or approval. The Cat nodded her head in agreement, and the others nodded back to her in relief.

Once Anthony was mostly dry on one side, the four of them turned him over. Dr. Daisy examined the cut in his side. It was not very long, but it was deep, so she quickly shaved the fur from around the area, applied some antibiotic cream, and put in four stitches while the others continued to dry him. Then, with the help of the handles on the tarp, they lifted him and moved him over to the mattress that was already covered with a warm electric blanket. Gently they rolled him over so that they could pull the tarp out from under him. Dr. D. hung an IV bag of warm fluid to help warm the dog from the inside while Suzanne put a mask over his muzzle to put warm oxygen into his lungs. Finally they put another warming electric blanket on top of him. Then all the humans stood back while Cleopatra took her place and curled up under Her Anthony's chin. Only then did Hakeem say to the doctor, "If you don't need us for anything else right now, I'd like to join my friend at the hospital."

"Of course," said Dr. D. "This would have been a lot harder without your help. Have you heard anything about the boy?"

"Yes," Jeffrey's uncle answered. "He seems to be stable and doing OK, but we won't know for sure until the next eighteen to twenty-four hours."

"It's going to be about the same for us too." Dr. Daisy put her hand on Hakeem's arm and looked him in the eyes. "It's going to be a long night for all of us. Thank you for your help. Now go and be with your friend."

⌇⌇⌇

When Hakeem arrived at the hospital, he found Michael, Michelle, and his wife, Tina, all sitting in Jeffrey's room. He looked over at the still, pale little boy lying on the bed and at all the equipment around him. All he could think of to say was "Well?"

His wife was the first to answer. "The doctor says that, all things considered, he's doing pretty good. We just have to wait out the next few hours."

Hakeem nodded. Taking a seat with his wife and friends, he said, "You know, I left Anthony with almost the same kind of setup—the blankets, the warm IV, and oxygen, and waiting out the next few hours. It all seems to be the same for both The Dog and The Boy." They all agreed. Then he turned to his wife. "So, I'm guessing that The Girls are with your mother."

"Yes, I called her right after I talked to you, and she came right over so that I could be with Mike and Michelle." Then Tina looked back at her friends. "I suppose that I should have asked this a long time ago, but Michelle, where's Bobby?"

Michelle Wilkinson's face turned red, and she looked down at her hands, away from both her friends and her husband. "Well, we don't know exactly, but we're pretty sure that he's someplace with Auntie Emma-Gene." Michelle had told her husband all this before others had arrived. Her husband had not been pleased, but he realized that this was not a usual situation. It was hard to go through it again and defend herself to her friends.

"OK, after the accident no one knew what was going to happen, and we didn't want Bobby to see it, so I took him back to the van, hoping that somehow, someone would eventually show up who I could leave him with. Auntie was already in the van when I got there."

Tina broke in. "Wasn't your van locked?"

Michelle shot back at her, "Of course, it was! The woman can show up in any house in Bowie, so do you really think a van is going to be much of a challenge for her?" After pausing for a moment to calm herself down, she went on, "Anyway, she said that she knew I needed her and that she was there to take Bobby home. You have no idea how relieved I was, Tina. This was someone whom we've all known all our lives. I thanked her, and as I turned to leave the van, and, of course, forgetting who I was talking to, I realized that she had no way to get into the house." Here The Mother stopped to look down at her hands again, and her voice dropped almost to a whisper. "But when I turned back, both she and Bobby were already gone."

Tina Price could hardly get her words out. "Both of them? Gone? Well, that was a good one even for her."

Hakeem could not hold back. "Well, have you at least called her?"

This time The Mother covered her face with her hands. "No, I haven't yet. They could be at our house, or her house, or for that matter any house in the state. Hakeem, I was just so worried about Jeffrey I kept telling my-self that at least I didn't have to worry about Bobby too because he was someplace safe with Auntie. I guess I do have to call now. We need to know, wherever they are—Bowie, New York, or cruising down the Nile—if she can give him dinner and spend the night with him."

⌒〟〒〜

"Well, of course, my dear, Bobby and I are at your house. Where in the world would you expect us to be?" On the phone Auntie Emma-Gene, whether talking to Michelle or anyone else, always seemed to shout, as if she were talking through two oatmeal boxes tied together with a string instead of miles of very expensive high-tech equipment.

"Yes, dear, he's already had dinner.

"What did he have?

"Well, let me see. It was peanut butter and jelly on a waffle with some ketchup. Then I think we added sardines, strawberries, and chocolate ice cream, and we found some of those red cherries in the fridge. It was delight-ful, and we both loved it.

"So, how are Jeffrey and The Noble Anthony doing?

"All right, so we should know more in the morning.

"Yes, yes, I understand.

"Now, of course, My Lady is with the Noble Anthony? Excellent. Then at least we'll know for sure that one of them will be fine.

"Spend the night? Of course, I always carry anything I might ever need in my purse.

"So you want to speak to Bobby now? All right.

"Give Jeffrey kisses for me, and tell him that Auntie will see him soon with real kisses and maybe something special from my purse."

The little round cantaloupe lady handed the phone to Bobby. He said, "Hi, Mommy."

Yes, I'm being a good boy.

"Uh-huh, Auntie is taking good care of me.

"When is Jeffrey and Anthony coming home?

"They're both in the hospital, but they'll be home soon?

"Mommy, when is soon?

"OK, Mommy. I won't forget to say my prayers. I love you too."

Bobby gave the phone back to Auntie Emma-Gene, and as soon as the good-byes were said, the little boy broke into tears. "Jeffrey and Anthony are going to die! Jeffrey and Anthony are going to die!"

Horrified and surprised as his outburst, the older woman scooped the boy up into her arms, carried him to the couch in the family room, and sat down with him on her lap. She held him close to her and rocked him back and forth while giving him kisses on top of his head, doing her best to console him. "Bobby, Bobby, what do you mean? What on earth would make you think a thing like that?"

Bobby tried to wipe his eyes and stop crying so that he could tell her. "My friend David, from school, his grandfather went to the hospital, and died. They're Jewish, and so they had to sit and shiver. And they had to have a fun-er-al too. Then everybody had to be sad and not play." His tears broke out again. "I don't want to have to shiver at a fun-er-al and not be able to play. Because it was my fault!"

This time Auntie sat him up straight and looked him right in the face. "Bobby, why do you think that what happened to Jeffrey was your fault?"

The boy's face was red and streaked with tears. "It was my fault. We were racing up the hill, and he beat me again. I *never* get to win! So I ran into him and pushed him, and instead of just falling down, he rolled down the hill. Now he's going to die in the hospital, and we'll all have to be sad, and I'll never be able to play again!"

Auntie pressed him against her chest and rocked him again, but this time it was because she did not want him to see her trying to hold back her smile. "Bobby, Bobby, my dear sweet little boy. You had nothing at all to do with what has happened to Jeffrey and Anthony today." Again she sat him up so that he could look at her. "Tell me something. When you woke up this morning, did you think to yourself, 'I'm going to hurt my brother this morning'?"

A very soft, quiet "no" came from the boy.

"And even when you pushed him at the top of the hill, were you think-ing, 'I want something bad to happen to Jeffrey and Anthony'?"

"No. I just wanted to win for once. Besides, Mommy said that we can't hurt each other because we're brothers and we have to love each other."

"Very wise woman, your Mother. Bobby, sometimes in life bad things just happen. We don't want them to. We don't plan for them to. And we certainly don't mean to hurt anyone, but they happen anyway. These things are called: Accidents."

Suddenly Bobby's tears disappeared, and he clapped his hands. "Oh, oh, I know! Like when I fell on my bike and got a boo-boo." He proudly pulled up his pant leg and pointed to the healed and now almost invisible spot. "Mommy kissed it to make it better, and she said that it was just a fall and not a bad accident at all."

"You are very right! Now Auntie is going to tell you a couple of things. First of all, right now, Jeffrey is taller and stronger than you are because he's older. So he's always had a head start on you, but I can promise you that, before you know it, you will be taller and stronger than Jeffrey. He will still always be The Older Brother, but you will be The Bigger Brother."

Bobby's eyes got bigger and bigger, and he looked at Auntie as if she had just told him that Christmas was going to happen every day. "Really, Auntie? I'm going to be bigger?"

"I promise you, Bobby, and I've never been wrong about a promise. Now, one more thing. Even now Jeffrey has always still tried to take care of you and to look out for you, hasn't he?" Bobby nodded. "Well, I think that the time has come for the two of you to look after each other. You are now old enough to begin to take care of him and to look after him some. Don't you think you should do that?"

The day was catching up with the little boy. His head had fallen back into the softness of Auntie's chest, and his eyes had suddenly become very heavy, but before drifting off, he managed to say, "You're right. I'll take care of Jeffrey. He'd better not mess with me, because I'm going to be The Bigger Brother."

Dr. Daisy was worried. Knowing that the doctor would be spending the night at the office, Suzanne had left to pick up something for them to share for dinner before she returned home. This gave Dr. D some time to sit by herself and think. It had already been several hours, and the Mastiff's temperature had barely gone up one degree. He should at least be at the low end of normal by now, which would be around ninety-nine degrees. So what was she doing wrong? What had she forgotten to do? The dog was healthy. He was well fed and cared for. Playing with The Boys had given him plenty of exercise, and he was not overweight for his breed and size. So why in the world was he not responding? The dog had worked so hard and given so much of himself for the child she could not—no, she would not—let him go.

Suzanne returned with their dinner, and the two women talked about their problem patient and his constant companion while they ate.

"OK," said Suzanne while running her hand through her recently turned snow-white hair. "This is what we've done so far. We check his temperature every hour. Thank goodness, The Cat has let us do that, because one of us looking like their own grandmother is enough." She gave a small laugh. "He's had warm blankets under and over him, and we've hardly increased his temperature. We've given him warm IV fluids to help rewarm his blood and warm oxygen to warm his lungs. So we're warming him from the outside and the inside. We've even given him massages to try to help with his circulation. Short of lying down with him to try to give him our own body heat, I can't think of anything else."

With a reluctant sigh, the doctor said, "Well, there is one thing that I've read about, but I want to hold off on that until I'm completely desperate, which will be in another few hours. I've read where, in a couple of cases like this, they've used a drug to increase the dog's blood pressure under the theory that getting the blood to move faster will warm it a little." The frustration was apparent in her voice as she continued, "Part of this makes sense to me, but he's already so exhausted I don't want to try it until I have absolutely no other choice."

"I know," replied Suzanne. "Weird cat or not, he's a great dog, and come to think of it, even the cat seems to be worried about him. If we're not doing something to him, she's right there with him. Sometimes it's almost like she's talking to him." Both women laughed at the thought. Suzanne went on, "See, I'm beginning to get a little crazy. Must be time for me to head home." Her voice softened. "I hate to leave you, but I really do have to go. I have faith in you, Dr. D. I'm certain that you'll figure something out. See you in the morning, and I'll bring breakfast and coffee."

After the two women had said their good-nights, Dr. D locked the door and returned to the back room, where The Noble Anthony lay covered in blankets with His Lady curled under his neck. The Cat's head was resting on the dog's big muzzle as if it were a pillow, and one arm was stretched out so it rested just above his eye, as if she had been petting him and soothing him, just as a wife would do for her husband. It was time to take his temperature again, but the doctor decided not to. If this was to be the end for the Big Dog, then let it come in peace. She could check it again in a couple of hours, but for right now she lay down on the floor beside them so that she could pet them both and listen to the soft song of Cleopatra's purr. After a little while, she got up and, while trying to read at her desk, fell asleep with The Mighty Trity in her lap.

Back on the floor of the exam room, Cleopatra woke, thinking that she had dreamed that she had felt Anthony move. No, it wasn't part of a dream; he had moved and was moving. "My Beloved, you are awake?" It was an exclamation and a question both at the same time. "Oh, My Beloved, My Anthony, you have come back to me!"

But the voice that spoke to her was not that of her big strong husband; it was that of an old, very tired dog. "My Lady, My Heart."

She could see his eyes moving and searching the dimly lit room full of strange smells.

"We are at Dr. Daisy's office, My Love," she reassured him.

"The Boy. My Boy, does he live? Will he live?"

"I have heard The Doctor talking to The Mother on the telephone." Her speech was slower now, more filled with caution. "The Boy has not awakened yet, but, they...they seemed to be encouraged by his progress so far." Trying to change the subject to something a little lighter, she went on, "Dr. Daisy has been here with that woman who was here with us before—Suzanne, I think her name is. But you know, I thought for sure that the last time her hair was darker."

It was the laugh of a tired old dog, but it was still a laugh. "Her hair was darker the last time that *we* were here." He stopped, and his body began to shake with chills. "Oh, I am so very cold. I can feel the warmth of the blankets under me and on top of me, but inside I still feel so horribly cold."

Cleopatra hooked one of the blankets with her claw and pulled it higher up around her husband's shoulders. "There, maybe that will help."

"My Love." Again it was the voice of an old, sick, and very tired dog. "I feel that I might fall asleep again, and in case it is The Forever Sleep—"

"No! No, no, no, do not say that! Do not ever say that, My Love." This time she threw her entire body against Her Anthony's face and wrapped her arms around it, hugging the huge face and head as best she could as she rubbed her face against his. "You are Mine, My Very Own, and I have marked you as such for all time."

Still shaking with chills, The Noble Anthony gave a deep and tired sigh and said, "I know, My Heart, but there is something very important that I must tell you while I still can." He paused for a moment, as if his strength was leaving him. "The two men. The men that I have been telling you about. The ones with the scent that I could not place. They were at the pond when The Boy and I were in the water."

"They were there? Among the crowd of people?" The Cat sat up now, and her eyes automatically searched around the room as if the men might somehow be there also.

"Yes. They were deep in the crowd, but My Lady, now I know who they are. I knew their scent, although I could not place it before. But we have indeed met them before, and now I know where."

"Anthony, Anthony, tell me, who are they?" There was an urgency in her voice, as if she was ready to run out and hunt them down at that very moment.

"They are the men from our time at The Temple, My Dear One. They are the ones who were at the house that horrible night. They are the men who killed me."

Cleopatra's eyes flashed a green that briefly filled the room, and when she spoke, her voice was a whisper. "How can this be, My Anthony? Those men would have died centuries ago. They could not be here in this time and in this place with us now."

"Yes, I know." His voice sounded even more tired now, as the stress of talking weakened him. Again he shook with chills. "You are right. Those men did indeed die centuries ago. The men who are here with us now are their children—no, I mean their descendants. From century to century, the men here now have descended from the family line of those very men." His voice was growing weaker. "I do not know if they plan to do us or The Family any harm, but you may have to be the one to protect The Family if I cannot." With that The Big Mastiff's eyes closed, and with a loud sigh, he drifted back into a deep sleep.

Cleopatra again bent down and rubbed her face against that of Her Beloved, marking him once again as hers and hers alone. Then she got up and walked over to the other side of the room, where she sat staring deep into the dark of the room, lit only with a small night-light. Still the green glow of her eyes filled the room, and this time her voice was strong and defiant as she called out, "Oh Mighty Bastet, Mother of us all, please hear my plea."

The Creature moved through the small room, which was made to feel even smaller by the size of the beast. It quickly found the sleeping Anthony and sat for a moment looking at him before hooking a giant claw into the blankets covering the dog and pulling them away, exposing the vulnerable animal. Slowly and gently it lay its much larger body on top of that of The Big Dog and wrapped its huge arms and legs around him, making its own body a living blanket of warmth engulfing The Noble Anthony. For a moment, probably from feeling the added weight around him, Anthony woke, but he felt no fear. In fact, all he felt was a calming and comforting warmth deep inside him that seemed to penetrate his entire body. He felt relaxed, loved, and cherished as he drifted back to sleep, hearing the special purr that His Beloved purred only for him.

Hours later, with the sunlight of the new day just beginning to appear through the windows of her office, Dr. Daisy woke with a jolt. She saw the light streaming into the room and then looked at the clock on her phone.

How had this happened? How had she managed to sleep so late? She had set an alarm on her phone. Why had it not gone off? She was supposed to have checked on the Mastiff hours ago. She jumped up, grabbed her stethoscope off the desk, and ran toward the exam room, not knowing what she would find. The doctor turned on the lights as she went through the door, and then she stopped still as she looked at the body of the dog lying on the mattress on the floor. Later she would take his temperature one last time, assuming Cleopatra allowed it, to confirm what she already knew. The Noble Anthony lay on his side with his mouth open just a little bit, and he was panting because he was *COOLING* himself.

Dr. D wanted to jump up and down in joy, but instead she held herself to a smile so big that it made her face ache. On top of Anthony, Cleopatra lay on her stomach with all four of her legs stretched out as if she was trying to make herself into a cat blanket around the huge dog. "Sure," Dr. Daisy thought. "A twelve-pound cat trying to keep a two-hundred-pound dog warm with its body. That is wishful thinking, all right."

The vet walked over and knelt down beside the two. Anthony looked up at her with what she was sure was a smile and a sleepy face. When the doctor ran her hand down the cat's back, she saw Cleopatra open one green eye open and look at her before closing it again, ready to return to her rest. Dr. D petted her again, saying aloud, "I don't know what there is about you because you are for certain one very strange cat, but all I can say is good work. Good work, My Lady."

⌒⑂⌒

Hakeem had needed to return to the Fire Station, but Tina had stayed with Michael and Michelle in Jeffrey's room. In some ways The Boy was better. His body temperature was up and getting closer and closer to normal. His color was much better, and he no longer had that scary blue-gray look. So far, there were still no signs of the black marks of frostbite on his fingers or toes. These things were good, but there were still no signs of him regaining consciousness. Though it was not bad, it was something to worry about. Tina Price looked out the room's window and could not believe that she was seeing the pinks and blues in the sky of a new morning. It had been a long night. She turned to her friends. "I'm sure that the cafeteria is open now. I can go downstairs and bring up some breakfast. As far as I know, neither of you had any dinner, so you must be starving by now."

The Father and The Mother looked from each other to their friend and shook their heads no. Then Michael said, "Tina, there is no reason for you to stay any longer. You've already been here beyond what anyone would expect, and I'm sure that your mom could use some help with The Girls by now."

Tina looked at her husband's best friend and laughed. "You're kidding, right? Mike, my mother knows why I'm here and who I'm with, and Hakeem will be here when he can. We're here for the duration, whatever that might be—a week, a month, a year. Except for the occasional shower and picking up a couple of changes of clothes, one of us will always be here with you and Michelle. When one of those doctors walks in, if he has good news, we're going to be here to celebrate it with you, and if the news is..." Jeffrey's godmother could not bring herself to say the words. "If the news is *not* good, then we'll be with you and cry with you if that's what's needed."

"Tina, you're being silly. Go home." The Father's voice was firm. Tina Price's voice was equally firm when she answered him. "No, Michael. I'm not being silly. I'm being a friend, and this is what friends do for each other. However long it takes, whatever happens, we will be here beside you, Michelle, and Bobby, because we are friends and we stand together no matter what."

There was nothing for Michael Wilkinson to do but put his arms around his friend's wife and hold her tight. "And to think that I tried my best to talk Hakeem out of marrying you."

All the adults looked at each other and laughed. They laughed a good laugh that they all needed until, peeping through the laughter, they heard a very small and weak voice say, "Mommy, where am I, and where's Anthony?"

Silence, and then all three of them ran to the bed and saw sleepy eyes looking up at them. "Oh, Jeffrey! Oh, My Boy!" was all The Mother cried, as she held his head in her hands and kissed his face over and over again.

"It's good to have you back, son," Michael said. The Boy's voice was hoarse and weak, and he looked around the room, completely confused. "I don't know where I've been, and I don't know where I am now. Hi, Aunt Tina. What are you doing here? Where is Anthony? I was falling down a hill, and he was trying to catch me, and—"

"Take it easy, darling. There's no rush. Your father and I will fill you in on everything that's happened." His Mother was smiling, with tears still running down her face. "And we have plenty of time to do it."

In a few minutes, The Boy had fallen back into a peaceful sleep. All the adults hovered over him as if he were a newborn whose every move had to be celebrated. The Mother looked over and saw Tina Price picking up her handbag. "Tina, you're not leaving now, are you?"

"Of course not. I'm going to go downstairs and get us all some breakfast so we can celebrate over coffee and orange juice." Tina stopped for a moment and took her friend's hand. "If I had left when Michael told me to and I had missed seeing those wonderful eyes open"—she nodded toward to The Boy—"I would have NEVER let Mike forget it."

The two women hugged each other, and Michelle said, almost crying again, "It would have been a much harder night without you and Hakeem being here with us."

"And if it had been one of Our Girls lying there, you and Mike would have been right here with us because we're..."Both women laughed a little in embarrassment because it came out a little louder than they thought it would when together they said, "FRIENDS!"

❧

The sky had grown dark again when The Mother and The Father heard a knock at the door. The familiar face of Hakeem poked around it.

"Uncle Hakeem!" Jeffrey called out.

"Hey there, Little Man. I'm glad to see that you're awake. I'd hate to think that I had snuck your friend in here for nothing." Just then the huge head of The Noble Anthony came through the door.

"Anthony! Come here, Big Boy! Come here, my Big Tony!" Jeffrey called to His Dog. The Boy could not hide his surprise when he saw that there was a wide band wrapped around The Dog. It met on the top of his back with a handle, which his uncle held in his hand. It held and supported The Big Mastiff as if he were a giant piece of luggage.

"Don't worry, Jeff. The Big Guy's legs are still a little weak from the cold of the water. He'll be his old self in a few days, but when I went to see him tonight, he wouldn't let me leave unless I brought him here."

The Boy watched as his uncle used the handle and guided The Dog over to the side of his bed. Then, supporting Anthony's middle with one hand, he lifted The Dog's front legs onto the bed with the other, while The Father lifted the back legs onto the bed beside The Boy.

"Oh, Jeffrey! Oh, My Boy!" Instead of giving the excited sloppy licks and kisses that His Boy had expected, The Big Dog quietly lay his huge head on His Boy's chest. "When we were in the water together, I could still hear and feel your heart beating even through all your wet clothes as you lay on my back. So I had to come to hear and feel your heartbeat again to be sure that you were all right."

Now it was The Boy's turn to cry as he hugged and kissed the big head covering his entire chest. "Oh, Anthony, you are the very best dog a boy could ever have. I love you, Anthony."

"And I love you, My Boy."

The adults stood at the foot of the bed, joyfully watching the reunion of The Boy and The Dog, when suddenly something occurred to Michael. "Hakeem, where's Cleopatra? How did you manage to get Anthony here without her? They're almost always together."

"Well, I do have a *little* pull in this place, you know." He straightened his firefighter's badge to show off his position of high authority. Seeing that no one was impressed, he continued, "The hospital actually didn't have much of a problem with it when I asked if I could bring Anthony in for a visit, especially since I mentioned that he was one of the heroes of Bowiefest. It seems that not only had most of the staff seen his and Scout's pictures in the paper and on TV, but they said that dogs can help people to heal better. Thinking that now they couldn't say no to me about anything, I made the mistake of mentioning Cleopatra. Unfortunately some of them had heard stories about her too. I tried to tell them that those stories couldn't possibly be true, but they still seemed to feel that everyone might be safer if she arrived in an animal carrier."

Once again the adults looked at each other and laughed as they said together, "And we all know that wasn't going to happen."

The Parents and Uncle looked back at the bed and saw that Jeffrey and Anthony had both fallen to sleep with their arms around each other. The Father spoke as he remembered all the dogs whom he had loved and who he knew for certain had loved him in return. "Cats are OK, I guess, but you know, sometimes A Boy just needs His Dog."

⌒⌒⌒

In a week everyone was finally back home together. Anthony arrived first and His Boy the next day. The Mother had planned a special celebration dinner for everyone. Even though Bobby had been to visit his older brother in the hospital, the younger boy still seemed completely enthralled with having him back home. Anything that he wanted, from a glass of water to his tablet with his favorite game on it, his younger brother would run and get for him. All this attention from Bobby was just too weird, so when The Parents were in the kitchen putting together ice cream and welcome-home cake, Jeffrey pulled his little brother close to him so that The Parents could not hear and said, "You know what happened wasn't your fault, don't you?"

"Oh yeah, I know that," came his brother's quick response. "Auntie Emma-Gene told me."

The older boy had not been prepared for that answer. "Well, OK. I just wanted to be sure that you knew because I didn't want you to feel guilty or anything."

"No, Auntie told me that it was an accident. She told me that an accident was something that we don't want or plan to happen but that sometimes they just do happen and that they are no one's fault. That's why we call them accidents."

Jeffrey was beginning to think that maybe he was the one who needed to have a talk with Auntie Emma-Gene so that she could explain to him what in the world was going on with his little brother. "OK, as long as you know. As long as you understand. OK?"

"Sure."

The evening went on with ice cream and cake. Then it was time for bed. And so began the tooth brushing, the baths, the story reading, and finally the prayers and kisses. When The Parents had left the room, Bobby got out of his bed and began to tuck in all of his brother's sheets under the mattress. Finally, Jeffrey could not take it anymore. He asked his brother what in the world was going on.

"Well, Auntie Emma-Gene explained everything to me. She said that as brothers we would always have to look out for and take care of each other. Auntie said that because you are the older brother, you are already taking care of me. But she also said, in fact she promised, that one day I would be bigger than you. So I thought that after what happened to you and Anthony, I couldn't wait until I was bigger. I had to start looking out for you and taking care of you, right now."

Jeffrey sat up in bed and called out, "Come over here." He then did something to Bobby that he had not done since the other boy was a baby. He took his brother's head in both his hands and kissed his brother on the head. Bobby immediately pulled away and began frantically rubbing at his head to try to get rid of his brother's cooties.

"What did you do that for?" he demanded.

Jeffrey snuggled down into his newly tucked bed and said, "It's just the way an older brother says Thank You to his bigger brother."

Bobby crawled into his own very untucked bed. "Well, OK, but don't say Thank You too often."

While The Boys talked, Anthony had moved into his place at the top of the stairs. Cleopatra took her place between his two log-like front legs and then turned and rubbed the side of her face against his three or four times.

"What was all that about, My Beloved?" he asked.

"To remind you to never leave me." She purred softly to him.

Then he answered, "With all my honor, I will do my very best to be forever at your side."

Strangers in the Night

One thing that was very nice about living in this part of Maryland was that it had a definite winter, spring, summer, and fall. There may not have been a lot of space or time between them, but they happened. That year the weather had been colder, and the winter had had a lot more snow than usual, but just a few weeks later, all the snow was finally gone, lawns were turning green again, little white flowers called early snow drops were blooming, and purple, blue, and yellow crocuses were popping up everywhere. The very early daffodils were beginning to show their little yellow heads, and the green stems of their taller cousins, the jonquils, were already standing six inches tall, getting ready for their turn.

The warmer days had people outside doing early spring cleanup in their yards and gardens. They were poring over new garden catalogs on kitchen tables, planning new flower and vegetable gardens. Fathers everywhere were already wandering around the big-box hardware stores looking over new grills and other equipment while complaining to each other, "Why do we look forward to spring so much when there is always so much work to do outside?" These would be the very same Fathers who would then rush home to their new grills or newly cleaned old grills and proudly cook the season's first hot dogs, hamburgers, steaks, shrimp, and fish—as well as *vegetables*, because The Mothers said they had to.

Spring—it was just a good and happy time. With both Jeffrey and Anthony being well and strong again after their unplanned dip into Fox Hill Pond, it was a pretty happy time at the Wilkinson household too. Several weeks ago The Noble Anthony had returned to his duty of escorting His Boys and the other neighborhood children to and from the school bus stop, with Cleopatra sitting once again in her place of honor on top of the Noble One's head. The Mastiff had also talked with Sniffer and some of the other local dogs about the two men whose scents had been in the neighborhood since the last The Pronouncement Day and Bowiefest. Even the Labrador and Golden Retrievers, who everyone knew were willing to play with anyone who would throw a ball for them, had been instructed to bark at the scent or sight of these men, even if they had a ball in their hands. All was good and safe for now, but all the dogs were on guard.

Eddie and Freddie Dansler were twin brothers who also thought spring was a great time. In fact, the two thought spring was a wonderful time for their business. In the spring people were happy and excited to be outside in the fresh air and warm sunshine, and sometimes that would cause them to be a little careless. Dad might forget to put away his tools or to lock the tool-and-lawn-mower shed that was in the backyard. A family running off to soccer practice might forget to close a door all the way, and, of course, during spring break many families would go away for a few days, leaving their homes empty and unprotected. That was just the time the brothers were waiting for because Eddie and Freddie were thieves.

The two men were proud of the fact that they came from a very long line of thieves and robbers. For as long as anyone could remember, for as many generations back as anyone could recall, most of the men and some of the women had made their living by entering other people's homes uninvited. Once inside they helped themselves to the things that other people had worked very hard for. At times they would even laugh and say that all families had their traditions and that breaking, entering, and stealing were theirs. So maybe it was a good thing that the Dansler family members were not very good thieves. In fact, half of the time, most of the family was in jail someplace, but that did not seem to keep them from trying.

Some members of the Dansler family even felt that from time to time, the twins had sold out because they had taken jobs, which within that family was almost unheard of. The twins had protested that they had only done so because the courts had required them to before they could get out of jail, and, as usual, they did not keep the jobs very long anyway. After all, when you had a job, there were all of these ridiculous requirements and expectations, like arriving on time, wearing clean clothes, bathing, being pleasant to customers and coworkers, not overstaying lunch or break time, and actually showing up to work. Of course, the most outrageous and completely unacceptable requirement of all was actually *doing the work* they were being paid to do. That was the deal breaker, for sure. Even so, many in their family of thieves and robbers still felt they were not holding up The Family Traditions. That was all about to change.

Over the years the Dansler twins had experienced several unfortunate incidents with small dogs. Many small dogs, though now loving lap pets, had started out being bred not only to hunt rats and other vermin but to actually dig and go into the burrows after their prey. It takes a dog with a strong heart and a lot of courage to do that, and so Eddie and Freddie had discovered that little dogs were no pushovers. First, the little dogs would bark like crazy, quickly waking their families to come and see what was going on. That did not usually end well. Then, to make matters so very much worse, little dogs could move very fast, and they would bite. They would bite hard, and they would bite often. More than one of the twins' trips to jail had come about when a small dog had bitten one or both of them so badly that they had no choice but to go to the local emergency room. Of course, each time the police had been put on alert and were there waiting for them.

That was then, but now they knew for sure it would never happen to them again. They now had what they had never had before—a PLAN. One night while watching TV (on someone else's TV, in someone else's home), the twins had come across the most wonderful and glorious TV program of all. It was called *Gentle Giants*. The show had been all about LARGE-BREED DOGS. It told them that, unlike their smaller yapping and biting cousins, gigantic dogs were just big quiet couch potatoes who wanted nothing more in life than a good tummy rub. They saw picture after picture of huge dogs sitting calmly with babies and small children. They saw them stretching out on couches, stuffing themselves into small chairs, trying to sit in the laps of their too-small humans, and pushing their humans out of bed.

This was it! This was all they had to do! From now on, they would only break into and rob the homes that they knew for certain contained *A REALLY BIG DOG*. After riding around the county for several months, they had decided that The City of Bowie had the biggest population of very large dogs. Tonight they planned to break into the home of the largest dog that they had ever seen. This dog had even been in the local newspapers and on one or two local TV shows. He was famous, and in turn they would be famous too. The Dansler twins slapped each other on the back because they knew for certain that their family would be telling the story of their triumphant escapades for many years and maybe even decades to come. Tonight, they were going to rob the home of The Big Mastiff called Anthony.

⌒⟋⟍⟍

Sniffer the Bloodhound, according to all the other dogs, had a sense of smell so strong that he could have described what kind of trees were on the moon, if there had been any trees on the moon. Sniffer would normally go into his backyard and howl long and loud at pretty much nothing or anyone, because that is what Bloodhounds do until their humans bring them inside to keep the neighbors from complaining. These days, the Bloodhound, with his painted toenails and with ribbons on his ears, howled to let all the other dogs know that the men The Noble Anthony had told them about were in the neighborhood more and more often. It was almost as if the men were looking or waiting for something.

Of course, then all the other dogs had to howl in response to let Sniffer know he had been heard and they were on guard. The community was suddenly full of howling dogs. Dogs like Anthony, whose family could not remember even hearing him barking before, now watched him sitting outside many times during the day and until the family went to bed at night, howling back and forth with all the other dogs. The human family could only shake their heads and wonder what in the world was going on with all of their dogs at the same time.

Cleopatra knew what was going on, and she did not like it. She had been staying closer to Anthony than usual since the unfortunate incident at Fox Hill Pond. The whole school had been abuzz because, even after Anthony was well again, she had still canceled a couple of Tea Parties with Gwen and Athena. She even went so far as to go and sit beside Her Husband during the frequent daily howling sessions. Once in a while, some people even thought that they might have heard a strange roaring sound mixed in with the dog howls.

It was the last day of school before Spring Break. The Wilkinsons' early-morning kitchen was full of the excitement and anticipation of the day trips and other activities that The Family had planned to do together. The Mother had been wandering in and out of the laundry room for some time now, waiting for Anthony to arrive with Cleopatra. It was beginning to get late, and The Mother still had to dress Cleopatra and watch her not eat and then attempt to bury yet another can of cat food. She was just about to call out to one of The Boys to find out what was keeping them when Cleopatra appeared and jumped up onto the counter, and she was alone. Michelle Wilkinson's eyes quickly darted around the laundry room, expecting to see The Big Mastiff once again trying to play hide-and-seek somewhere as a joke, but this was no joke. Anthony was nowhere to be found. The Mother looked back at Cleopatra, and the green light that flashed between them was so strong the woman took several steps backward, putting her hand out to catch and support herself on the counter behind her.

"Of course. I understand." That was all The Mother could manage to say before she left the laundry room. When Michelle Wilkinson reached the kitchen, she clapped her hands together a couple of times to get the attention of her husband and sons. "Anthony is not feeling well and will not be taking the children to the bus stop this morning."

The male members of The Family looked at her as if she had suddenly begun speaking a different language. Anthony, not take the children to the bus stop? He had only missed two weeks after The Unfortunate Insolent At Fox Hill Pond, because Cleopatra had threatened to tell The Mother to put him in a DOG CRATE if he tried to leave the house.

The Father put down his paper. "Is he sick? Should we call Dr. Daisy?"

"I don't know yet. I'm going to go upstairs and check on him, but for right now, Jeffrey and Bobby, you go and get the first group of kids and bring them to our house. Your Father will meet them here and go with you to collect the next group on the way, and he will see everyone safely onto the bus." Michelle turned to her husband. "Michael, by the time you get back, I will have seen Anthony and Cleopatra, and they will have told me what to do from that point."

"Mom, is Anthony really sick?" Michelle could hear the worry and concern in her eldest son's voice. All His Mother could say to him was an honest "I don't know, son. I know that you're worried, so I'll tell you what. As long as you don't hear from me, everything is OK. But Jeffrey, sometimes big dogs can get something that's called a twisted stomach. It can happen very fast, and it can be very dangerous, but I promise you, if it's something bad, I'll come get you at school so that you can be with him. Just remember, if you don't hear from me, he's OK. Besides, I think Cleopatra would have let me know if it was really something to be concerned about."

In the past when his wife would say something about her communications with Cleopatra, Michael Wilkinson would have rolled his eyes and looked up at the ceiling, giving the "oh, not that again" look. Since The Family's experiences at Fox Hill Pond, he did not know why, but The Father found that he was not as quick to dismiss these interactions between His Wife and Cleopatra as he used to be. So this time, he only motioned to The Boys to get moving, and then he went out to the garage to make sure the back of the van would be ready if Michelle needed it for a ride to the vet.

The Mother went upstairs and found The Big Mastiff at his post at the top of the stairs, lying down with his head resting on his two big front paws. She sat down on the floor beside him and stroked his head while two big, sad, blue-brown eyes looked back at her. "What's the matter, Big Boy?" she asked him. "Are you having a bad day?"

She stopped petting him for a moment so that she could feel his ears to see if they felt warmer than usual to her. His ears felt fine and just as puppy soft as usual. Next she touched his big nose. It was cool and wet, so without getting a thermometer, The Mother did not think that Anthony had a fever. Next she pulled down the lower lid of one of his already droopy eyes. She was looking for anything that might look yellow, which could mean that there was something wrong with his liver, but everything seemed pink and healthy. She tried again by pushing back his big jowls in order to look at his gums for the same reason. Still nothing. The Mother sighed, and not knowing what to do next, she took one of his big puppy-soft ears in her hand and shook it gently and lovingly.

"OK, Anthony, you won't talk to me, but you also don't seem to be in any pain, which would be a sign of twisted stomach, so we've reached the end of my vet knowledge. I'll let you have today, but if you're not up and playing with The Boys or walking the neighborhood with Cleopatra on your head by this time tomorrow, we're going off to see Dr. Daisy. Rest now, and I'll bring you a Puppy Cookie later." With that, Michelle gave her Big Mastiff a kiss on the head and went back downstairs.

Cleopatra, who had been sitting and watching everything from her bed in the linen closet, jumped down and sat next to Anthony. "Why did you not let me tell her what is happening? Now she is just worried about you."

Anthony lifted his head and gave His Wife a big wet lick across her face just because he knew that it would annoy and distract her. "I did not want to tell the humans because I do not know anything for sure. I only know I had to have some reason to stay very close to the house today. Sniffer howled last night that the two men were close, very close. He also said that their scent was different. They were sweatier, as if they might be excited about something. Maybe it was because of something they are going to do, but that is still nothing that I can tell the humans. They know nothing about these men."

"But if you let me tell her, The Mother will believe me," The Cat said reassuringly.

"Once again, My Beloved, what would you tell her? That there are two bad-smelling men in a white van in the neighborhood? No, we can only wait and see." Anthony ended with another big wet kiss, and this time his very wet wife gave him a bop on the nose with one of her paws, which made them both laugh.

⌐ᴖᴗ

The Father left work early that day so he could meet the school bus. As the bus pulled up to a stop and the door opened, all the children came pouring out, and those at the windows were shouting the same thing at him: "Is Anthony all right? What about Big Tony, Mr. Wilkinson? Mr. Wilkinson, tell us, is Anthony OK?"

Michael asked the kids to quiet down so that he could talk to all of them and the bus driver at the same time. "Anthony seems to be doing OK, but if he's not back to being himself by tomorrow, we're going to take him to see Dr. Daisy, just to be on the safe side." The bus driver conveyed the message to the rest of the children in the bus before pulling away. As The Father began his walk to deliver the children to their homes, he watched his two boys run ahead of everyone else straight to their house, while in the background he heard what had become the familiar sounds of howling dogs.

Both Boys burst through The Puppy Door and then through the laundry and into the kitchen, where The Mother was. Before they could start on their list of a thousand questions about Anthony, she simply pointed and said, "Sunroom."

As Jeffrey and Bobby ran in that direction, dropping backpacks and jackets along the way, they could see The Noble Anthony lying on the floor on his side with Cleopatra sitting on the couch above him. Jeffrey, of course, arrived first and immediately slid in beside His Big Dog, putting his arms around him and resting his head on Anthony's. Bobby had to make himself content with Anthony's back, but he still put his arms around The Dog and found a soft spot on the back of Anthony's head for his own. Thankfully, The Big Mastiff was a Two Boy Dog.

Jeffrey petted the big head as tears threatened to fall. "I worried about you all day. You get better; you hear me?" The Boy sat up a little. "Do you feel like you might want to go outside and play some?" The only answer The Boy received was a look from big sad eyes. "You're right; dogs are making too much noise outside anyway, so suppose I read to you? Would you like that? What do you want me to read?"

Bobby sat up and shouted out, "How about *Lassie*? Anthony loves *Lassie*."

"Quiet!" Jeffrey said, in full older-brother mode. "Anthony's the one who doesn't feel well, so it's his pick. When you're sick, it can be your pick."

The Noble One wagged his tail so that it beat against the floor and said, "I would love to hear *Lassie Come Home*."

Bobby, taking little-brother triumph wherever and however he could, simply made a face at his brother before quickly taking cover behind Anthony again. Jeffrey got up and returned with the book and then sat down on the floor again, but this time he put his back up against the couch for support and comfort—and so Cleopatra could see the pictures from her seat above him on the couch. Anthony moved over just enough to rest his head on His Boy's lap and, of course, dragged Bobby along with him. Jeffrey cleared his throat and began reading. "Everyone in the village knew Sam Carraclough's Lassie. In fact you might say that she was the best known dog in the village..."

Michelle Wilkinson glanced up from preparing dinner when she heard Jeffrey's voice, and she thought she was looking at the most perfect picture of dog, cat, and boys that she had ever seen. Life was good, if only those dogs outside would stop howling.

⚞⚟

Eddie was driving Freddie, his younger brother by two minutes, crazy. All day they had been watching the house but moving their van so that the neighbors or the police would not notice them. All day Eddie had wanted to check their equipment again and again, even though Freddie had told him a gazillion times that not only did they have all their equipment, but also if they had any more, they would not be able to carry anything out of the house. All day Eddie had wanted to go over their *PLAN*, again and again. Now Freddie had a headache, and it was only being made worse by the almost constant howling of the neighborhood dogs. So Freddie could hardly believe it when his brother turned to him and said, "You know, I think we're ready."

"Are you sure?" Freddie hoped that his voice sounded mocking.

This had been completely lost on the older brother, who continued in all seriousness, "Yes, this time I'm really sure. We're going to go into that house. We're going to find that big lazy dog on the floor or couch someplace, just like the TV said. Then I'm going to offer him a ball, if he's a ball kind of dog." He pulled a brand-new tennis ball out of his pocket, held it up, immediately dropped it, and had to scramble to find it on the messy and dirty floor of the van. Finally he held the ball up in triumph—though it was now accessorized by several candy-bar wrappers—before quickly stuffing it back into his pocket. "Then, if he's not a ball kind of dog, you're going to give him A Puppy Cookie. No dog can resist them." Eddie looked at his younger twin and waited—waited for him to show his Puppy Cookie. "So!" he almost shouted as he pushed at Freddie. "Where's your cookie? What did you do with your cookie?"

Freddie bit his lower lip and hung his head while he reached into his jacket pocket and finally pulled out a broken piece of Puppy Cookie. The cookies for big dogs were usually about the size of the saucers placed under the cups when Grandmother comes over. The piece that Freddie held up was the size of a quarter.

"What in the world is that?" This time Eddie really was shouting. "What happened to your cookie?"

Freddie could feel his face glow red with embarrassment. "Well, they call them cookies, so I wanted to see what they tasted like. I suppose I got a little carried away because"—now his voice perked up—"they are really good! You should try them, Eddie! I wish I had another one."

Eddie could not control himself this time. He took off his baseball cap and began to hit his brother on the head with it. "You numbskull! You could have spoiled our entire PLAN. Suppose he's a cookie kind of dog and you've eaten all the cookies? Then what am I supposed to do? I should offer you to him and see if he's willing to eat you instead." The older twin gave his brother one more good swat with the cap just because. "Fortunately for you I know what a dimwit you are, and I brought extras." Eddie reached into his backpack, pulled out another Puppy Cookie, and held it up in front of his brother's face. "And if that big dog wants a Puppy Cookie and I see one bite missing out of this one, well, well..." His voice lowered as he tried to sound menacing and scary. "Something very horrible is going to happen to you."

"What, Eddie?" Freddy was almost whimpering. "Tell me what horrible thing is going to happen to me?"

Knowing that he had his brother truly frightened, Eddie would only whisper, "It's so horrible that I can't even mention it."

The Dansler brothers sat in silence as they watched the last light in the house go out. According to their PLAN, they had to wait at least another hour to be sure everyone in the house was sound asleep before they went in. They only heard one last howl from Sniffer before his humans made him go inside and stop making all that noise.

~~~

After Sniffer's final howl for the night, The Noble Anthony sat up from his place at the top of the stairs. He had put Cleopatra into the linen closet some time ago, to keep her safe. He had been smelling the strong scent of the men all night, and he knew they were in a van parked right in front of the house. As long as the men stayed in the van, everything would be all right. The night was quiet now, and Anthony's ears perked up, listening for every sound. Listening, listening, and then he heard it. The click of a van door opening and the soft sound of someone trying to close it as quietly as possible. Anthony jumped up immediately and went to Cleopatra's shelf in the linen closet.

"My Lady, My Lady, wake up. The men are out of their van, and they are heading toward the backyard. You stay here while I go and wake The Parents."

Cleopatra was awake and on her feet in a second. "No, you stay on guard, and I will wake The Mother."

"My Darling." Her Husband was trying to be patient, but his annoyance still came through in his voice. "I know that you have great skills, but we do not have time for you to stare at The Mother until she's awake like you usually do!"

Sitting on the bed beside The Mother and staring at her until she awakened was always Cleopatra's preferred method. It actually worked surprisingly well; it just took a rather long time to do it. Fifteen minutes or an hour, she could never be sure.

"No, no, I can do this. I have another way that is much faster. You need to stay in case they come in and come up the stairs. I promise I'll get her." Without another word she jumped from the shelf and ran down the hall toward The Parents' bedroom while Anthony returned to his post. Cleopatra leaped onto The Mother's side of the bed.

The Mother was lying on her side breathing softly, as The Cat had expected. Quickly she stepped onto The Mother's leg and walked the length of the woman's body until she reached the shoulder. She sat down for a moment before bending over and putting her cold wet nose right into The Mother's ear. Then she purred. The Mother sat up so quickly she knocked The Cat from her shoulder to the edge of the bed. It was the glint of green in the dark room that told Michelle that Cleopatra was with her. Still feeling startled and sleepy, The Mother held her hand up to her ear to try to warm the cold spot. "My Lady, what are you do—" She had no time to finish. The room instantly filled with a bright green flash. "Oh my goodness." She reached out and began to shake her husband awake, keeping her voice low. "Michael, wake up! Wake up now!"

A sleepy, grumpy-faced Michael Wilkinson turned to his wife, but before he would say anything, her hand covered his mouth. "Be quiet," she whispered. "Two men are breaking into the house. Anthony is on guard at the top of the stairs."

The Father opened his mouth to ask through his wife's fingers how she knew this, but then he saw a glint of green coming from the side of the bed. Without another word he got up and grabbed his bathrobe from the foot of the bed. In the dark shadows of the night, he could see his wife, already in her robe and with the portable phone in hand, leaving their room and heading down the hall to their sons' room. She was already following the one plan from The Family's list of what to do The Father had hoped they would never, ever have to use.

The Mother stepped into the Boys' room as quietly as possible, hoping that somehow they would be able to sleep through whatever was happening downstairs. First, she turned the lock on the door handle; then she stood on her toes so she could reach the sliding lock at the top of the door. After that she reached down so she could do the same thing to the one at the bottom of the door. She remembered she had secretly laughed at her husband when he had installed the locks. He had told her, "They're to slow down anyone who might be trying to kick down the door. It might give you and The Boys extra time to get down the ladder and get away." At the time she had given him the usual wifely eye roll, but now she was going to have to thank him for thinking to give them this extra level of protection and, if needed, time.

She had gone along with the folding ladder that dropped over the windowsill and down the side of the house because Hakeem had said it was for fire safety. If the stairs were somehow blocked, they would have another way to leave the second floor. It was The Father who had quickly added that it could also be used to escape bad guys. Now The Mother glanced at the box sitting neatly under the window and prayed that she would not have to use the folding ladder tonight. Still trying not to wake The Boys, she walked into their closet, almost twisting her ankle as she stepped on who knows what on the closet floor, and dialed 911. She spoke to the dispatcher as quietly as possible. She gave her name, address, and phone number and then told the dispatcher that two men were breaking into their home and how many people were in the home. She was surprised by the dispatcher's last question: "Mrs. Wilkinson, are there any firearms or weapons in the home?"

"Well, no. Why would you ask that?"

"Mrs. Wilkinson, most robbers don't carry weapons or firearms because the penalties are higher if a crime is committed with them. But if you or your husband should have one, we don't want the responding officers to harm either one of you by mistake."

"And I want to thank you for that. All my husband has is a baseball bat," The Mother said, almost laughing.

The dispatcher replied, "Now stay where you are." Then there was a short pause. "Is this the home of The Big Mastiff and that strange cat?"

"Why yes, yes it is."

The Mother was about to ask how they would know that, but before she could, the dispatcher, with a new sound of urgency in his voice, said, "Mrs. Wilkinson, the patrol cars are on their way."

Eddie and Freddie were almost shaking and giggling with delight. This time they had really invested in their profession. Sure, they had not gone as far as to get one of the big handles with suction cups on each end like those construction workers use to install and remove large panes of glass for windows. One of those was way too big-time and expensive for them, but Mastermind Eddie had decided that the kind of suction handle used in showers or bathtubs would work just as well for what they wanted. Their PLAN was brilliant, if Eddie did say so himself. Both the family room and sunroom had sliding glass doors. Each door was one large sheet of glass from top to bottom. Most of the time in such situations, they would use a glass cutter to make a circular hole in the glass near the lock so they could reach in and unlock the door and then slide it open. That was getting harder to do. Some new doors now had extra foot locks on them, or people would put some kind of bar in the door's track to keep it from sliding open. Also, a lot of the doors now had double panes of glass, so they had to cut through twice. When they pushed out the circle of glass, sometimes it would fall on the floor, make a lot of noise when it broke, and wake someone up. That someone was usually a small, barking, biting dog. People were making it harder and harder for The Thieving Dansler Twins to make a dishonest living! Still, Eddie Dansler felt that with this PLAN he would show them he was smarter. Not only would his family be talking about this for years to come, but they would also write and sing songs about them!

The PLAN was working perfectly. Freddie had wet the caps of the shower handle and pressed it against the glass door. He held it in place perfectly while Eddie used a glass cutter he had found on a TV shopping show. He was careful at the corners, making sure to cut around them and not into them, so the glass would come out more easily. When he had finished, he took hold of the handle with his brother, and together they pulled the entire sheet of glass out in one piece. They were about to dance with joy when they remembered they had to be quiet. They lay the glass down on the deck and detached the handle. Freddie pointed toward the door and held up two fingers to let his brother know there was a second pane of glass. Eddie made a thumbs-up sign, knowing that since this one had come out so easily, the other one was sure to do so also.

They began the whole process again. Freddie held the handle to the glass, and Eddie did the cutting. Just as they had done before, they both took hold of the handle and pulled. Nothing happened. The two men looked at each other and pulled again. Still nothing. Freddie looked angrily at his brother. "Are you sure you cut it all the way around?"

"Of course, I did," he whispered. "I'm not an idiot like you." Still he got the glass cutter out of his pocket and went around the edges of the door again. Once again they pulled, and once again nothing happened. "OK. Let's try pushing it this time." They both took a firm hold on the handle. "This time we're going to give it all we've got. So on the count of one...two...three!"

This time all they had was a bit too much. The glass gave way, and both men, taken completely off guard, fell through the opening. They were still holding the handle and sheet of glass as they all crashed to the floor. The sound of falling men and shattering glass was almost deafening. The two men jumped up as quickly as they could while trying to brush off pieces of broken glass and get their bearings in the dark room at the same time. Freddie reached into his pocket and pulled out his piece of now-broken Puppy Cookie. He held it out, calling, "Here, dogie. Here, big doggy, doggy. Uncle Freddie's got a Puppy Cookie for you."

much as Eddie wanted to take off his cap and hit his brother with it until his arm was too tired to do it anymore, he did not. He knew the big dog had to be in the house someplace, and all this noise would have it either running to see what had happened or running to hide under some bed, depending on how brave the dog was. He kept quiet and listened, but there was no sound in the entire house except for their own heavy breathing. Eddie reached out in the dark room to find his brother.

Feeling Freddie's arm, he grabbed hold of it, saying, "Come on, let's grab what we can and get out of here."

They had only moved a little farther into the room when they heard BIG, THUNDEROUS footsteps coming down the stairs. They tried to turn to run, but before they could move, a blinding green light filled the room, and all the Dansler Twins could do was scream.

With his wife locked in the bedroom with The Boys, Michael Wilkinson and his baseball bat went and stood at the top of the stairs with Anthony. He hardly noticed Cleopatra sitting beside The Mastiff. He absentmindedly rubbed the top of Anthony's head as he listened to the muffled sounds coming from the back of the house. Finally he bent down and whispered to Anthony, "OK, Big Boy, we've talked about this before. If these men should get into the house before the police arrive, as long as they stay downstairs, they can take anything they want. If they start to come upstairs, then they'll have to face you, me, and Bat Boy here." He gently tapped the bat against his leg. "Above all, we keep Michelle and The Boys safe, right?"

The Father had led his Big Mastiff through this several times. If anything like this should ever happen, Anthony was supposed to be the first line of defense at the top of stairs. Anyone coming up those stairs would walk right into two hundred pounds of snarling dog with a lot of big teeth. If they somehow managed to get past The Dog, then it would be up to The Father and Bat Boy. Both The Man and The Dog knew they would fight to death if they had to in order to keep Their Family from harm. Suddenly both The Man and The Dog jumped as the house filled with the crashing sounds of falling men and breaking glass. Anthony stood up and braced himself for battle. Michael Wilkinson slowly backed down the hall until he was just a few feet away from the room where his sons slept and his frightened wife sat waiting.

Cleopatra turned to Anthony. "The men are in the house now, My Beloved." She could smell their familiar, awful scent and hear their sneaky, creeping footsteps.

"Yes, My Lady," Anthony said without moving.

"These men whose ancestors harmed you before are now here and could possibly harm you again." This time her voice could only be described as being filled with cold determination.

Still not turning to look at her, The Noble Anthony responded, "Not now, My Lady," as he tried to focus on what he might be called to do.

This time Cleopatra's voice sent a chill down Anthony's back, forcing all his hair to stand on end. "This will not happen again! *BAAAASSSTTTET!*"

She screamed out the name as she shot in front of Anthony and leaped down the stairs. An automatic reflex made Anthony move one foot as if to follow her, but three thousand years of duty made him stand his ground and only whisper to her, "Be safe, My Beloved. Be safe."

⚞⚟

The Father, who was several feet back in the hall, raised his arms to protect his eyes from the blinding green light he had seen once before. This time it seemed to fill the entire house. The light went out, and even before he could think to begin to lower his arms, the screaming began downstairs. Like some horrible, never-ending nightmare, the sounds went on and on.

Terrible sounds of furniture crashing, breaking, banging, and clattering. The sound of some wild animal yowling and growling, fighting to protect its home and family. The begging and pleading sound of frightened men screaming into the dark at the top of their lungs, calling on their god for help. "Oh, please Sweet Mother of God, make it stop!" Followed by more sounds of breaking and crashing furniture, more begging and pleading, and then... silence. That was when The Noble Anthony left The Father and ran down the stairs and into the family room.

The Mastiff's eyes had no trouble adjusting to the darkness of the family room. This was his home, and he knew every item in every room by sight as well as scent. He paid no attention to the two men sitting on the floor in the corner huddled together, shaking and crying, as he maneuvered through the pieces of overturned furniture and glass on the floor. Instead, his attention was focused on the huge, hulking shadow with the blazing green eyes lurking near the door. For a moment he stopped, turned, and lifted his head. The sounds were still too far away for any human to hear, but the whine of the police sirens told him they only had a couple of minutes at best.

"My Lady, your actions tonight have put you in grave danger, and we have only moments before the police arrive."

A low snarl came from the direction of the glowing eyes.

"Please, My Beloved, follow me over here. The couch has been overturned, and you can hide behind it until you are..." Anthony stopped, choosing his words carefully so as not to agitate The Creature. "Until you are more yourself. But please, My Dearest, we must hurry."

The large shadowy beast moved slowly but followed The Mastiff to the hidden location. It lay down behind the overturned couch just as flashing red and blue lights appeared, coming up the street toward the house. With his Beloved out of sight, Anthony went over to stand by the two cowering and crying men in the corner and made what he hoped was a menacing face. He could hear the sounds of the police officers moving cautiously around the sides of the house. He already knew the officer to enter the house first would be The Family's friend, Chip Jacob.

Officer Jacob had gone to high school with Michael and Michelle. They had attended each others weddings, and their children were close to the same ages and went to the same school. He was thankful that calls like this one, in which someone entered a home in the middle of the night, did not come very often, because he never knew what he might find when he walked in. Getting this kind of call for the home of someone he knew just made it that much worse. With flashlight in hand and gun drawn, the officer walked slowly and cautiously around the side of the house and onto the ground-level deck. His light landed on the large panel of glass that had been cut out of the sliding glass door and that now lay on the deck. Then he panned his light up onto the door and saw the new entrance that had been cut into it. As he stepped through the opening, his attention was immediately drawn to the sounds of whimpering coming from inside the room. He hollered out, "In here, guys," to the other officers, who were still outside, while trying to hold back a laugh.

Every police officer in The State Of Maryland knew, or had heard of, The Dansler Twins, but Chip Jacob was pretty sure that no one had ever seen them like this before. Tonight the two were huddled in a corner, whimpering and shaking as they clung to each other, while The Noble Anthony held them in place. Since everyone in Bowie knew Anthony, he approached The Dog with a certain amount of confidence, saying, "Well, hey there, Anthony. It looks like you have already done most of our job for us. If they had only taught you to read these guys their rights, I'd be out of a job. But right now I need you to back away so the other officers and I can take over."

As the other police officers entered through the new opening in the family-room door, Anthony backed away, and Freddie and Eddie suddenly came to life. "Oh, thank goodness, you're finally here!

"We thought you'd never get here!

"What took you so long? We thought we were going to be killed!

"You have to arrest these people right away!"

"Hold on a minute, you guys. We find you two breaking and entering into a home that is not yours, and you think that we should arrest *them*?" This time the officers did not even try to hold back their laughter.

"Well, yes, of course!" Eddie went on in righteous indignation. "There has to be some kind of law about keeping a creature like that in someone's house. It could have killed us and the entire neighborhood. Those big green eyes that just glowed in the dark and the horrible sounds that it made!" Finally, realizing no one was taking him seriously, he grabbed hold of his brother and pushed him forward, shouting, "Look at him! Look at both of us! You don't think that we did this to ourselves, do you?"

The beams of six police flashlights now shone on Eddie and Freddie, and they were a mess, to put it nicely. Their clothes were torn—no, more like shredded—so deep that parts of their skin and underwear were showing. Red scratches, though not deep enough to draw blood, appeared all over them, and they were covered with long, thick, reddish-golden-brown hairs.

One of the officers cast his light over the rest of the room. "Chip, I think that you should take a look at this."

Chip Jacob panned his flashlight slowly over the rest of the room and let out a long, slow whistle. It looked as if every piece of furniture, every chair, and every table had been overturned, and there were deep gouge marks in them. Stuffing from cushions and pillows covered the floor as it a blizzard had exploded in the family room. There were also deep claw-like scratches on the walls, and everywhere there were these long thick hairs. Officer Jacob turned to the Dansler Twins. "OK, guys, this is bad even for you. Stealing from people is one thing, but you didn't have to trash the house like this."

The Twins immediately tried to interrupt. "But, but—"

"Save it for the judge, guys. Let's read them their rights. You would think by this time they would know them by heart themselves," the officer said to the others.

Over the years and decades to come, The Dansler Twins' family members would talk about the escapades of that night. Stories would be told and passed down from generation to generation. Many, many songs were written and sung. And there was laughter. Lots and lots of laughter. The night itself and the family history that they left behind had not been the legacy that they had planned. But based on their legend, it was rumored that several family members did find real jobs and were very successful in them.

～⋙～

Relieved to be hearing the voices of the police officers, Michael Wilkinson had been able to relax a little as he stood in the hallway outside his sons' bedroom. The Wilkinson Family Plan was that he should stay in place until he received the all clear from the police, so it felt very good to hear the voice of his high-school friend say, "Hey, Mike, it's safe for you and The Family to come down now."

"OK, Chip, just let me check on Michelle and The Boys first."

Of course, all the sounds of the crashing furniture, combined with the screeching, yelling, and screaming, had awakened The Boys. After His Wife had unlocked the door, Michael Wilkinson was not at all surprised to see they had all been huddled together in Jeffrey's bed. "Come on, boys. Officer Chip says that all the excitement is over. The bad guys have been caught, and we can all go downstairs now." As he bent down to pick up Bobby, he saw the worried look on his wife's face and gave her a small kiss on the cheek while he whispered to her, "It's all right, Hon. Chip wouldn't have told me to come down stairs if it wasn't safe."

"Dad, Dad, what about Anthony? Is Anthony OK?" The concern for The Noble One appeared on the faces of both The Boys.

"I'm sure that he is, or Officer Chip would have said so, but let's go downstairs and see for ourselves."

Both boys shouted with pleasure when they saw their Big Dog sitting at the bottom of the stairs waiting for them. Many hugs and sloppy Mastiff kisses were shared all around. Even though, much to Michelle's relief, the Dansler Brothers had already been removed to a police car, nothing could have prepared The Family for the carnage that had been done in their family room. One of the police officers tried to console them.

"Sorry about the damage, folks. It does happen; sometimes they just go crazy and trash the place. But I've never heard of these two guys doing this before." The officer paused a moment before continuing almost to himself, "I still don't understand all the scratches and hairs all over the place."

Michael Wilkinson had to agree with the officer. Yes, the room looked bad, with the overturned furniture and pieces of broken glass all over. Chairs and pillows were ripped or torn, and the huge claw marks had been made by something with a foot way bigger than Anthony's, but what really caught his eyes were the hairs. This was not the first time The Father had seen the reddish, golden-brown hairs. He had seen them at Dr. Daisy's, at Bowiefest, and now in his own home. There was something going on here. The Father just did not want to think about what it might be. Fortunately Officer Jacob gave him a much-needed distraction.

"Mike, Michelle, I hate to have to bring this up, but the Dansler Brothers kept going on and on about being attacked in here by some huge creature with glowing green eyes. I know it sounds ridiculous even for them, but I still have to ask. Do you folks have any kind of strange or exotic animals in here besides Anthony and, oh, well, that cat?"

"Oh, come on, Chip. All we have are the dog and the cat. Those scratches on the wall were made by some knife or something. Even Anthony's feet aren't that big. And as for Cleopatra...where is Cleopatra, anyway?" Michael looked around the room and saw Anthony sitting beside the overturned couch. Leading the officer behind him, he went on, "She must be here, hiding behind the couch like most cats would do."

When they got to the couch, there was a very exhausted-looking and limp Cleopatra stretched out on the floor behind the couch. Thinking, "Please don't hurt me. Please don't hurt me," the Father reached down and picked up the cat to prove his point. "See, Chip? There's no way even Cleopatra could have done all this. Even though she does have green eyes."

The officer laughed with his high-school friend. "You're right, of course, Mike. I just had to ask."

A couple of the officers righted the overturned couch, and Michelle sat there with The Boys. Michael gently placed Cleopatra in her lap. Then he turned back to Chip to ask, "What is all that noise out there, and where did all those people come from this time of night?"

Officer Jacob laughed and slapped his old friend on the back, saying, "That, Mr. Wilkinson, would be your neighbors."

༺ॐ༻

On a quiet street, in a quiet neighborhood, in a small city, blue and red flashing lights and sirens in the middle of the night are going to draw a crowd. Once the word got out about what had happened, some people were asking what they could do to help while others had already started. Mrs. Watson had brought over two big thermoses, one with hot chocolate and the other with her famous Cat Nip Tea. Mr. Dodd, who had an upholstery business, had left a note saying he would gladly redo their torn and ripped furniture for only the cost of the fabric, with no labor charge. A couple of men had shown up with plywood and tools and were already closing up the new "entrance" The Dansler Brothers had made into the family room. One lady, whom The Father was not sure he knew, had managed to find a broom and was sweeping up some of the glass scattered all over the floor. Someone else, whom The Father had only seen in passing, pressed a gift card from one of the big-box hardware stores into his hand, saying that her family had received it for Christmas and had not used it yet, and she was sure the Wilkinsons could use it more. There was even a text message from Hakeem saying he was sorry he could not be there. He promised to be there to help put in the new door and said that Tina and The Girls would bring over plenty of food for dinner that night.

After a while, Michael went back inside and found Michelle and The Boys still on the couch. He told her to leave Cleopatra and took the Family outside to see what wonderful and caring neighbors and friends they had. The sun was beginning to come up by the time everyone left. Mrs. Watson's hot chocolate had been wonderful, but now they were all feeling exhausted and ready for some sleep. The Mother and The Boys had gone upstairs to get blankets and Sleep Over Bags, as The Boys liked to call them, because none of them wanted to go back upstairs or to be far from each other. The Father had gone into the kitchen to put the hot-chocolate mugs into the dishwasher, and he saw Cleopatra sitting on the counter as if she was waiting for him. He looked at The Cat with her gold hoop earrings, her wide Egyptian-style collar, and, of course, her huge green eyes. Slowly he reached out and stroked her back. Then he bent down so he could be at eye level with her and said, "I don't know how, and I may not even want to know how, but I do know for certain you had something to do with all this tonight. I never thought I wanted or even needed a cat, but, Cleopatra, I want to thank you for protecting My Family tonight." Cleopatra bent over and gently rubbed the side of her face against The Father's, marking him as her own.

Later, when The Boys were all snuggled on the floor in their Sleep Over Bags, The Noble Anthony joined them gently pushing himself in between them, making what The Parents liked to call "An Anthony-and-Boy Sandwich." Michael and Michelle were snuggled together under a pile of blankets when Cleopatra jumped onto the couch. The Mother smoothed out the blankets on her lap to make the required place for her. Cleopatra walked onto The Mother's lap and marked the woman's hand, but then she went and sat on Michael's much more rumpled lap. As they watched

Cleopatra curl up and make herself comfortable on The Father's lap, the two humans looked at each other as if Martians had just landed. Slowly and tentatively, Michael Wilkinson reached out to pet The Cat and felt her body relax and almost seem to melt into him with peace and comfort. He felt his own breath inhale deeply and then exhale slowly as his body relaxed to the sound of special purring that was just for him.

After all the humans were asleep, The Noble Anthony moved over to take up his temporary guard position by the patched family-room door. His Lady Cleopatra soon joined him.

"You know you put yourself in grave danger tonight, My Lady."

Cleopatra leaned against her big Mastiff husband and then reached up so that she could mark the side of his face. "Yes, I did, but you are all safe, and everything is as it should be...for now."

Free Gift

Thank you for reading The Noble Anthony and His Lady Cleopatra. I hope you enjoyed their adventures. As a thank you gift you can get a free preview of their next book, *The Noble Anthony and His Lady Cleopatra Return Home*. *Visit the author's website www.paulettegaineswood.com/freegift*

Dedications

After many successful years in the publishing industry, Marion Ross decided to teach high-school English as her retirement job. I was fortunate enough to have her for both my sophomore and junior years. At a time when many schools thought that students should read aloud in class, she let a withdrawn dyslexic girl know that reading to yourself was perfectly acceptable because it was the *reading* part that was the most important. She also let that same young girl know that even though spelling and writing were almost impossible for her, it didn't mean that she had no stories to tell. Mrs. Ross left this life many years ago, but her friendship and teachings will stay with me forever. She was a wonderful bright light in a very dark time for me.

The next person I met who believed that I had stories to tell became my husband. All through our marriage of almost thirty-five years, George H. Wood has listened to and encouraged me to write down my stories. He has been a fan and supporter of *The Noble Anthony and His Lady Cleopatra* from the very first time he heard about the cat who traveled around on the head of a dog. He has listened patiently as their stories grew and their world expanded. He never gave up on them as characters whom children and adults would enjoy, and he never gave up on my ability to tell their story. These are his stories as much as they are mine.

Acknowledgments

As we all know, it does take a village, a community of family and friends, to raise a child. I have discovered that it takes that same village to produce a book, because without their love, support, and encouragement, *The Noble Anthony and His Lady Cleopatra* would still just be stories rolling around in my head. Athena S. Cochrane—whose loyalty and devotion to her friend helped me to define what friendship is. Jena Cochrane—the gift of a daughter whom I never knew that I wanted or needed but whom the universe gave to me anyway. I will never stop being grateful for this wonderful gift.

Loryn Austin—fun, laughter, and friendship.

Alyssa Holleran—the best-ever plan-B saving angel.

The entire congregation of St. Matthew's United Methodist Church of Bowie, Maryland.

The Bowie Volunteer Fire and Rescue Department.

The Bowie Police Department

The entire population of Bowie, Maryland.

Every dog and cat whom I have ever met or owned or who has owned me. They don't know or care about all the things that we as humans worry about so much: Does my boss like me? Have I gained five pounds (or fifty)? Will this outfit impress anyone? They only know that you have returned to them each day so you can love them and be loved by them—yes, even the cats.

About the Author

Paulette Gaines Wood lives in Bowie, Maryland with her husband George. They have three cats. None are Abyssinian, but they all came from rescue shelters already pre-loaded with strong individual personalities, shedding, purring, and love.

Please enjoy coloring this picture of The Lady Cleopatra.

Then, with your parents' permission and help, post it on your Facebook page and share it with us on our page, at https://www.facebook.com/TheNobleAnthonyandHisLadyCleopatra

Please enjoy coloring this picture of The Noble Anthony.

Then, with your parents' permission and help, post it on your Facebook page and share it with us on our page, at https://www.facebook.com/The-NobleAnthonyandHisLadyCleopatra